THE POETIC ART OF
# A. E. HOUSMAN

# THE POETIC ART OF
# A. E. HOUSMAN

## Theory and Practice

B. J. LEGGETT

University of Nebraska Press
Lincoln and London

*Publishers on the Plains*

UNP

Copyright ©1978 by the University of Nebraska Press

The publication of this book was assisted by a grant from The Andrew W. Mellon Foundation.

**Library of Congress Cataloging in Publication Data**

Leggett, Bobby Joe, 1938–
    The poetic art of A. E. Housman.

    Includes index.
    1. Housman, Alfred Edward, 1859–1936—Criticism and interpretation. 2. Housman, Alfred Edward, 1859–1936—Aesthetics. I. Title.
PR4809.H15L4    821'.9'12    77–15792
ISBN 0–8032–0969–X

MANUFACTURED IN THE UNITED STATES OF AMERICA

FOR Will AND Leslie

# CONTENTS

# PREFACE

THE CHAPTERS WHICH FOLLOW attempt a revaluation of A. E. Housman's stature as an artist. In the process they consider a number of related issues—Housman's fate at the hands of the New Critics, his conception of poetry, the links between his theory and practice, the relationship of his view of art to those of more influential modern poets, the presence in his poetry of a theory of art which is now identified with Freud and contemporary psychoanalytic criticism. My purpose in dealing with these issues is quite simply to clarify Housman's conception of his own art and to demonstrate the vitality of both his theory and craft. I have devoted a great deal of discussion to the thematic and formal elements of Housman's poetry, but by far the most attention is directed to his theory, for it is here that he has obviously been most vulnerable as an artist.

Although this is a topic which has not been dealt with at any length, no commentator can escape the influence of earlier scholarship, and my indebtedness to published Housman criticism is acknowledged as fully as possible in the footnotes which follow each chapter. It is difficult to single out individual critics for special consideration, but I should mention three whose names occur here more frequently than any others. Christopher Ricks has compiled the collection of critical essays which offers the most balanced view of Housman, and I have frequently referred to his own essay on the nature of Housman's poetry, as well as to his introduction to the collection. Cleanth Brooks, one of the most influential critics of our time, I have used (I hope not unfairly) as a spokesman for the formalist views which have had a good deal to do with Housman's present reputation. Finally, I am indebted to Norman Holland for his version of a psychoanalytic theory of poetry I have detected in Housman.

Two chapters were published separately in slightly altered versions, and I am grateful to the editors of *Modern Language Quarterly* and *Victorian Poetry* for permission to reprint materials in the third and fourth chapters. I am also grateful to Holt, Rinehart and Winston for permission to quote from *The Collected Poems of A. E. Housman,* 1965. Finally, I must express my appreciation to the University of Tennessee Graduate School and to the John C. Hodges Better English Fund of the University of Tennessee English Department for providing the summer grants through which much of this material reached its final form.

THE POETIC ART OF
# A. E. HOUSMAN

# 1
# INTRODUCTION

CRITICS ARE NOT GIVEN to demeaning their own craft, yet criticism has in numerous ways helped to remind us of its limitations. The very transience of critical theory, the inability of widely held tenets to rule more than a few decades, is one reminder of the frailty of our trade. Another is to be found in what is perhaps the most common convention of the modern critical essay—the notion, more often implied than stated directly, that all previous criticism on a particular issue is mistaken and is now being corrected once and for all. We suffer this convention, I believe, because like others it embodies a truth, and the truth is not that impressions of a writer's art are easily corrected but rather that they are inevitably, from some point of view, misleading. In a sentence deleted from the final version of *The Name and Nature of Poetry* Housman offered a simple and surprisingly apt explanation for the critic's dilemma: "Not only is it difficult to know the truth about anything, but to tell the truth about anything when one knows it, to find words which will not obscure it or pervert it, is in my experience an exhausting effort."[1]

Given the difficulty of the critic's task and the fallibility of his methodology, it is not surprising that practical criticism has become, in the main, an endless process of correction, and the commentator is faced with the prospect that his own corrections are subject to the same process. These observations, as random as they may appear, are pertinent in several ways to what follows. The conception of criticism as an im-

1

perfect and severely limited tool is, first of all, the keynote to Housman's pronouncements on the art of poetry, and it is reflected as well in some of the assumptions implicit in the chapters that follow. Moreover, this study is itself an attempt to correct what has seemed to me a misleading impression of Housman as an artist. I thus find myself employing the overworked convention to which I have just referred, although I have tried to avoid giving the impression that all previous thought on Housman is mistaken or that I am correcting it once and for all. In addition, the issues of Housman's conception of art and his stature as an artist are quite closely related; there is little doubt that the present estimates of Housman's reputation as a poet are based to a large extent on the supposed anti-intellectual conception of poetry and criticism with which he is identified and with his efforts to counter the view of poetry which was ultimately to dominate the first half of the twentieth century.

To offer an estimate of Housman's present reputation is itself a dangerous enterprise, yet it is not so difficult to summarize the popular stereotype of Housman the poet. (One of the marks of the minor poet must be the ease with which he lends himself to stereotyping.) In his introduction to a collection of modern essays on Housman,[2] Christopher Ricks attempts such a summary, and it serves quite well as an illustration of the issues I am addressing here. Ricks captures admirably the faint note of condescension which the "highbrow" critic feels for Housman. He points to the widespread notion that Housman's poems are nothing more than the literature of those who don't really care about literature—maiden aunts, old-world dons, and the very young. He reminds us of the gift-book status of *A Shropshire Lad* which classes it with the *Rubáiyát of Omar Khayyám* and the poems of Kahlil Gibran. And he isolates the word which must be familiar to every Housman critic: *adolescent.* The image which emerges is that of an old-fashioned ("classical") poet who has been made popular by the middlebrow reader and who is associated with donnishness, nostalgia, and the sensibility of adolescence.

Ricks's attempt to account for Housman's present image centers on the two aspects of his poetry with which we are all familiar—the simplicity of his verse, which has led to its popularity with the "wrong" kind of reader, and the supposed adolescent appeal of his poems, which disqualifies them in the minds of other readers as subjects for serious attention. Yet while he is certainly correct in pointing to the surface simplicity of Housman's verse as one of the chief factors in modern judgments of his stature as a poet, Ricks's emphasis on the nature of the poetry alone does not go quite far enough in explaining Housman's precarious hold on modern readers. For one thing, as Ricks admits, Housman's poetry has been praised by such highbrows as William Empson, Randall Jarrell, and Cleanth Brooks, critics who should not be attracted to the simple and the merely popular.

If, however, we observe the kind of praise Housman has received at the hands of such critics as Brooks and Jarrell, the case is not so inconsistent as it first appears. Brooks, for example, is able to defend the poetry only by separating it from the poet, who is the object of one of Brooks's harshest attacks in *Modern Poetry and the Tradition*. In several instances he makes clear that the finest qualities of Housman's poetry stand in direct opposition to the picture Housman presented of himself as an artist and poetic theorist. Similarly, Jarrell's appreciative essay "Texts from Housman," as its title indicates, isolates the texts of the Housman poems it discusses; the poet as a conscious artist is hardly present. And Jarrell goes so far as to suggest that Housman was not himself responsible for the most intriguing implications of one of the poems—the notion that our actions are motivated by the wish for death, and that our apparent reasons for acts are merely rationalizations: "But I am not going to hold up Housman's poem as a masterly anticipation of our own discoveries; so far as I can see, Housman was not only uninterested but incapable in such things, and pulled these truths out of his pie not because of wit, but because of the perverse and ingenious obstinacy that pulled just such gloomy judgments out of any pie at all."[3] This is an attitude characteristic of New Critical discussions of Housman's poetry. By such an account, Housman's finest moments are chance products of perversity and obstinacy; the poet stands responsible for them in only the most oblique manner.

There is ample evidence (and I have attempted to provide it in this study) that Housman's reputation as a poet has been based on a consensus that runs as follows: Housman was a naive and eccentric poet who, almost by accident, produced a significant body of verse based on a wrong headed theory of art. He was hopelessly out of touch with his own time, and his poems succeed, when they do, almost in spite of his own conception of his craft. He was, in other words, the poetic innocent, the writer who may be largely disregarded in charting the course of literary history since he had no lasting influence, no relationship with other poets or with the literary temper of his own age. We may find variations of this view echoed in the statements of such influential tastemakers as F. R. Leavis and the other *Scrutiny* critics, I. A. Richards, C. Day Lewis, and Louis MacNeice. It is implicit in Ezra Pound's opinion that Housman was apparently unaware of the world of his contemporary poets and in Cleanth Brooks's attacks on Housman's conception of poetry in *Modern Poetry and the Tradition* and elsewhere. The notion of Housman as the naive, popular poet who does not require the critical scrutiny accorded his contemporaries is perhaps best summed up in an exchange reported by one of my colleagues several years ago. A doctoral student who announced to his professor that a note on a Housman poem had been accepted for publication was taken aback by the rejoinder that Housman was not the kind of poet about whom one published critical articles.

Underlying the various reasons that may combine to eclipse the reputation of an artist is usually the dominance of a critical school or theory which is unsympathetic to the conception of art which he represents. This fact is rather obvious, yet it is frequently overlooked for the simple reason that a critical conception or methodology, formalism for example, may so dominate the sensibilities of its adherents that they can conceive of no other legitimate way to approach a body of literature. Thus, one might point to the lack of complexity in Housman's poetry as a critical problem without recalling that such virtues as complexity, paradox, and tension are of fairly recent vintage, promoted by a conception of art expressed earlier but not widely held in the academy until the forties. Yet once it achieved its hold, no method of criticism has so deeply permeated the hearts and minds of readers as formalism in all its variations, with the result that its practitioners by and large regard it not as a current school of criticism but simply as the manner in which one reads literature. This belief is no doubt true to some extent of the followers of any critical dogma, yet formalist theory presents an interesting complication. Its less doctrinaire elements (close, careful reading texts; attention to structural patterns and unity) may indeed be thought of as the manner in which one reads literature; yet its assumptions about the nature of literature and criticism (the critic as Ideal Reader, the self-sufficiency of the text, the centrality of paradox and irony, for example) are rather more problematic and are already showing signs of their advancing age.

The dominance of formalism and related theories which assume that criticism is an intellectual exercise based on ascertainable criteria and performed on the literary text has had more to do with conditioning our present estimate of Housman as a poet than with our judgment of his poetry. Although such a statement may seem inconsistent, the distinction between poet and poetry is important because of the peculiar fate Housman has suffered at the hands of modern critics. While many of his poems have been condemned for their sentimentality, lack of ironic detail, and threadbare texture, some have been singled out for praise in terms of their wit, paradox, and daring conceits, and enough have been salvaged to warrant the conclusion that his verse has narrowly survived the scrutiny of New Critical methodology. Yet almost without exception the influential critics—formalist and otherwise—who have considered Housman's whole conception of poetry, his theory of art, have dismissed him as the "naif poet"—the designation of C. Day Lewis—or painted the picture, as Cleanth Brooks has done, of the natural genius hampered by a simple minded notion of poetry. It is significant that both Day Lewis and Brooks admire much of Housman's poetry (for different reasons), yet they find themselves unable to credit the poet for the effects they admire. The consequences of this approach are predictable:

Housman has become a poet whose verse is appreciated but who has never gained much respect as an artist. It is for this reason that a concentration on the nature of Housman's poetry alone can never fully answer the questions raised in examining his place among twentieth-century poets.

If one had to point to an event more responsible than any other for the present low estimate of Housman as an artist, it would be the occasion of his Leslie Stephen Lecture, *The Name and Nature of Poetry*, delivered in May, 1933 and published the same month. Seldom has such a mild, scholarly document created more protest, and I can think of no other poet so nearly universally damned for his conception of poetry. Reasons for the continuing hostility to Housman's theory are not hard to find. He had the misfortune to advance an anti-intellectual conception of poetry at a moment when scientific and intellectual theories were just reaching an ascendency they were to maintain for the entire time that Housman himself was to be appraised as a poet. If he had deliberately chosen to alienate the critics most responsible for twentieth-century tastes (and there is reason to suspect that his choice of targets was deliberate) he could not have secured a better opportunity. He was, in fact, so successful in articulating his opposition to the very foundation of modern criticism—the application of intellect, method, and established criteria to the literary text—that his reputation as a serious artist has never recovered.

For not quite half a century Housman has been so obviously wrong about poetry that no one has bothered to examine his views in any detail, to study them in the light of the critical climate of his time, or to apply them to a full-scale study of his verse. Then, too, outside of *The Name and Nature of Poetry* and his own verse, Housman had little to say about his art. There has therefore been no apparent reason for a comprehensive examination of Housman's whole conception of poetry, that is, a concentration on Housman as a serious artist as opposed merely to an examination of his poetry or, more frequently, of selected poems. Several considerations, however, make such an examination desirable. In the first place, the critical assumptions which he argued against in *The Name and Nature of Poetry* have now become sufficiently diffuse to allow us to consider such heretical notions as the inessential nature of metaphor and the purely subjective state of literary evaluation. This is not to say that Housman's assumptions about poetry may now be proven valid, his opponents' invalid. But it is now easier to argue that Housman's views deserve to be examined as rigorously as those he attempted to counter.

A second consideration is the desirability, in my own mind at least, of rehabilitating Housman's reputation as an artist. If it can be shown, for example, that the best of Housman's poetry follows from his conception of art, it will no longer be possible to adopt the condescending attitude that his verse was a happy accident or to imply that it succeeds in spite of his notions about poetry. The formalist tendency to separate the poem from the poet has had the effect, in Housman's case, of simultaneously preserving the poetry and obscuring (or damning) the poet. But it is clear that the reputation of any important poet depends on more than the close reading of individual poems. Yeats, Eliot, Pound, Williams, Stevens represent for us not writers of discrete poems but artists for whom the theory and the practice of poetry were inseparable. The fact that Housman has not achieved the stature of this distinguished group does not deny the principle that the art of a poet must be seen in its broadest sense, including the poet's assumptions about the nature of poetry and its creation, his view of his own place in the tradition of poetry, and his defense of his own style and subject matter. This is only a way of saying what is obviously true: the concern with a poet's art cannot be confined merely to examinations of his poetry based on the critic's conception of art. Although that is itself an indispensable enterprise, it gives us primarily a sense of how a body of poetry fares under a current theory of art or, perhaps, a sense of how valuable the critic's methodology is in dealing with a body of poetry.

We may, of course, talk about the art of a poet in any number of ways, most of them vague or ill-defined, but in the sense that I am using the term it involves more than the craft of constructing poems; it encompasses the theoretical scaffolding upon which the poems are constructed as well.

Ultimately, an examination of a poet's art must take into account the general issue of the poet's place in a broader conception of poetic art derived from tradition in addition to the more specific issue of the relationship between his own theory and practice. Housman's poetry has not suffered from the lack of a sympathetic hearing so much as Housman as a poet has suffered from our image of him as the Sunday painter of poets, the gifted amateur whose art was so limited as to be negligible.

The alternative position is not to claim that Housman was a major artist whose concept of art wrought significant changes in twentieth-century poetics. However, there is a great deal of room between the two positions of gifted amateur and major artist. Because Housman went against the prevailing tendencies of modern poetry and poetics, he has served criticism thus far only in a negative way, as the straw man or the example of wrong headedness. I believe that he has more to contribute to our understanding of modern literary history and the formulation of poetic theory. Even if we conclude that Housman had little to offer to twentieth-century poetry and poetics, one valuable result of examining his contribution should be a greater understanding of his own theory and practice.

This study, then, is an examination of the elements of Housman's art which have appeared most questionable to twentieth-century commentators. Since the questions which have been raised about his poetry and poetics are related directly to formalist assumptions about poetry, the chapter that follows offers a specific case of one New Critical appraisal of Housman. By concentrating on the judgments of Cleanth Brooks, a critic who has become perhaps the best-known practitioner of formalist methodology and who has written widely and not altogether unsympathetically on Housman, I hope to clarify the position I have already stated here and to locate more exactly the points of contention between Housman and the generation of critics who have been most influential in arbitrating his case. The third chapter provides an extended discussion of the primary source of these points of contention, *The Name and Nature of Poetry*. My primary intent here is to provide an account of what

Housman actually said in this crucial document, as opposed to the positions which are attributed to him. But I also wish to examine the assumptions that underlie the infamous pronouncements of the lecture and to trace some of the sources of these assumptions in nineteenth-century poetic theory.

Because the relationship between Housman's theory and his own practice as a poet is still in question and because the supposed inconsistency between theory and practice has cast some doubt on his integrity as an artist, I have devoted two chapters to aspects of Housman's poetic practice which may be linked to the notions voiced in *The Name and Nature of Poetry*. Chapter 4 argues that the tone, voice, and point of view which characterize Housman's verse are directly related to his nonintellectual theory of poetry. Chapter 5 extends this link to the structural patterns which dominate his poetry. These chapters are not, however, devoted exclusively to the poems as embodiments of poetic theory. Although they suggest links between theory and practice, they also attempt to appraise the most characteristic elements of Housman's poetry as products of a highly developed craftsmanship. The well-known account of the origin of his poetry Housman provided in *The Name and Nature of Poetry* has fostered the impression that his poems appeared ready-made in his head, and this impression of utter artlessness is abetted by the ingenuousness of his persona. A moment's thought and a look at the manuscript revisions should have been enough to disabuse readers of this notion, but the commentator who would treat Housman as a serious artist is still forced to counter the idea that he is the naif poet in practice as well as in theory.

The sources of our present opinions of Housman and what he represents have their true beginnings in the thirties, when the most influential poets and critics as well as journalists and reviewers were beginning to take sides in the continuing debate between traditional and contemporary tastes in poetry. Publication of *The Name and Nature of Poetry* placed Housman for a time in the center of this debate, which I have attempted to examine in chapter 6. Such an examination reveals what we might have suspected—that Housman was seen as the adversary of contemporary trends

in poetic taste as represented by a poet and critic like Eliot
and that both Housman's attackers and defenders tended to
read (or misread) his statements on poetry in light of an
imagined battle between Housman's Old Guard and Eliot's
Reactionaries. In the heat of battle some important distinctions were obscured and critical positions were blurred. It is
only through a chance occurrence—the almost simultaneous
pronouncements by Housman and Eliot on the same
subjects—that these misconceptions, which have persisted
to the present, can be corrected. My contention—that Eliot
and Housman take essentially the same position on the significant issues raised in The Name and Nature of Poetry, that
they reach substantial agreement on conceptions of criticism, questions of meaning, and descriptions of poetic
composition—would no doubt have seemed absurd to a critic of the thirties, and it will initially seem so to a critic of the
seventies. Yet a comparison of Housman's Leslie Stephen
Lecture and Eliot's Charles Eliot Norton Lectures supports
such a view, and although the parallels say nothing about
the validity of Housman's theory of poetry, they say a great
deal about the misconceptions which have followed his
statements on poetry to our own time.

Since it is located principally in his verse, Housman's
conception of his own poetry is somewhat more difficult to
evaluate than his more general statements of poetic theory.
One important indication of his view of the function and
value of his poetry has been not so much misconstrued as
ignored. I am referring to the poet's apologia which is contained in the two concluding poems of A Shropshire Lad and
stated most explicitly in the penultimate poem "Terence,
this is stupid stuff." Here Housman asks and answers a question which is obviously central to his own art and which has
intrigued theorists from Aristotle to Norman Holland: what
is the value of a poetry which exhibits only the darkest and
most painful aspects of our human state? Chapter 7
examines the implications of Housman's theory of what I
have called the mithridatic function of poetry, and it does so
both in relation to classic statements of the issue—that is,
Aristotle, Matthew Arnold—and more recent attempts to
formulate a theory of the manner in which literature trans-

forms the painful and the unpleasant into something acceptable and even desirable. It may seem surprising (although it should not be, given a theory which defines poetry as a nonintellectual transfusion of emotion and locates its origins in the unknowable depths of the mind) that the closest correlates to Housman's conception of the ultimate value of his poetry are the theories of Freud and contemporary Freudian critics. Although Housman anticipated it by more than two decades, Freud's *Beyond the Pleasure Principle* provides the theoretical background for Terence's defense of his poetry, and later amplifications of Freud's theory by such critics as Lionel Trilling, Ernst Kris, Simon O. Lesser, and Norman Holland testify to the significance of Housman's contribution to a classic problem in aesthetic theory.

In the concluding chapter I have indicated some further implications of Housman's view of the function of his own poetry and of poetry in general. I have tested the mithridatic theory against his own verse and suggested links between this early view and many of the characteristic elements of his poems. I have also attempted to tie together some of the various strands of theory and practice which make up this study. But not too neatly, I hope, for the acknowledgement of the limitations of criticism derived from Housman's approach to poetry warns us of the danger of mistaking informed opinions for immutable truths. No reading of a poet is final. In endeavoring to correct the received opinions on Housman's status as an artist I have no doubt provided the opportunity for countless future corrections of my own approach. Yet my purpose will be served if the ensuing rectifications generate fresh discussions of a poetic art which has been too easily dismissed.

## Notes

1. Henry Maas, ed., *The Letters of A. E. Housman* (Cambridge, Mass.: Harvard University Press, 1971), p. 335.
2. *A. E. Housman: A Collection of Critical Essays* (Englewood Cliffs, New Jersey: Prentice-Hall, 1968), pp. 1–10.
3. "Texts from Housman," *Kenyon Review* 1 (1939):271.

## 2
# HOUSMAN AND THE MODERN
# READER: *The Issue of Metaphor*

HOUSMAN'S JUDGMENT IN *The Name and Nature of Poetry* that simile and metaphor are "things inessential to poetry"[1] is so inimical to twentieth-century formulations of poetic theory, which generally assume the centrality of metaphor, that the reader may be surprised to discover that the statement was written in 1933, when presumably the poet should have known better. Such a conception of metaphor, if voiced in the nineteenth century, would merely sound old-fashioned; offered in the third decade of the twentieth century, it has the ring of heresy. Yet it is a part of a theory of poetry which finds its real expression in the early decades of the nineteenth century and is one indication of the peculiar position which Housman occupies in the tradition of British poetry—a modern poet of Romantic heritage whose view of metaphor does not differ greatly from that of, say, Wordsworth. Both poets share the opinion that the intellect can be harmful to the poetic imagination, and metaphor, a product of the intellect, has for Housman a status similar to seventeenth-century wit, which always runs the danger of becoming "intellectually frivolous" (SP, p. 173), a designation which is roughly comparable to the Romantic category of the fancy.

Since Housman's conception of poetry obviously has some bearing on his own practice as a poet, as well as on his unique place in the tradition of late nineteenth and early twentieth-century poetry, it is worthwhile to attempt to fix its position in relation to other conceptions of the nature of poetry which have influenced his own view or against which his view must now be judged. I shall attempt the former task in the following chapter; at present I am concerned with modern judgments of Housman's poetics.

It is difficult to choose a spokesman for the moderns, but I take it there is general agreement that the formalist critics have exerted the most influence on the manner in which we now read poems. Certainly they have done the most to discredit the view of poetry promoted in *The Name and Nature of Poetry*, the one document which gives anything approaching a comprehensive account of Housman's poetics. Rather than compile a list of modern reactions to Housman's conception of poetry, I should like to use one of the most articulate and eclectic of the formalists, Cleanth Brooks, as representative of a point of view which has dominated criticism for a good part of the twentieth century. Brooks has written at some length on Housman's view of metaphor as well as on his verse, the former in *Modern Poetry and the Tradition* and the latter in a lengthy essay published in the *Kenyon Review* in 1941 and in the Centenary Lecture on Housman delivered at the Library of Congress in 1959. His remarks are illustrative of what appears to be the prevailing judgment of Housman's status at the present time, and the issue of metaphor is, as in so many other aspects of modern theory, central.

It is understandable that Housman should be taken to task by Brooks for his remarks on metaphor, for in *The Name and Nature of Poetry* he violates two of the most sacred tenets of Brooks's formulation of poetic theory—the essential nature of metaphor in poetic statement and the importance of wit, which "far from being a playful aspect of the mind, is the most serious aspect."[2] It is, in fact, Housman who bears the brunt of Brooks's attack (in *Modern Poetry and the Tradition*) on the uncritical reader who must be shown that "the play of the intellect is not necessarily hostile to depth of emotion" and who "must discard the view that wit is to be associated with barren and shallow ingenuity."[3]

I am not attempting here to argue the validity of Housman's conception of metaphor, although I do wish to clarify it. The issue was long ago decided to most people's satisfaction in Brooks's favor. The question which seems to me of more immediate interest involves the relationship of Housman's view of metaphor, and the conception of poetry that prompts it, to modern assumptions about poetry. It is a part of a larger question which concerns the very nature of Housman's poetry and its place in the British poetry of the early twentieth century; but that is too imposing a question to allow for a simple answer, and one must be content with getting at it through a series of more manageable ones. It may be well to begin by clarifying Housman's conception of metaphor in *The Name and Nature of Poetry*; Brooks's reconstruction of it seems to me a bit misleading. The theory of poetry of which it forms a part is almost purely Romantic. The fear of the intellect, the emphasis on poetry as the transfusion of emotion, the hatred of poetic diction, the distrust of wit or any intellectual device which would interpose itself between the poet and the expression of human feelings— these are the heritage of Wordsworth's 1800 Preface, advanced by a poet who regarded Wordsworth as "the chief figure in English poetry after Chaucer" (SP, p. 109). It is in this context of what M. H. Abrams and others have termed the expressive theory of art that one must view Housman's statement on metaphor which Brooks finds shortsighted, a shortsightedness, incidentally, which, in Brooks's view, Housman shares with two centuries of critics.[4]

Both Brooks and I do Housman an injustice by quoting his statement on metaphor out of context. The passage in *The Name and Nature of Poetry* in which the assertion occurs is quite helpful in explaining Housman's hostility to the conception of metaphor which Brooks has helped to advance:

There was a whole age of English in which the place of poetry was usurped by something very different which possessed the proper and specific name of wit: wit not in its modern sense, but as defined by Johnson, 'a combination of dissimilar images, or discovery of occult resemblances in things apparently unlike.' Such discoveries are no more poetical than anagrams; such pleasure as they give is purely intellectual and is intellectually frivolous; but this was the pleasure principally sought and found in poems by the intelligentsia for fifty years and more of the seventeenth century. Some of the writers who purveyed it to their contemporaries were,

by accident, considerable poets; and though their verse was generally inharmonious, and apparently cut into lengths and tied into
faggots by deaf mathematicians, some little of their poetry was
beautiful and even superb. But it was not by this that they capti-
vated and sought to captivate. Simile and metaphor, things inessential to poetry, were their great engrossing preoccupation, and were
prized the more in proportion as they were further fetched. They
did not mean these accessories to be helpful, to make their sense
clearer or their conceptions more vivid; they hardly even meant
them for ornament, or cared whether an image had any independent power to please: their object was to startle by novelty and
amuse by ingenuity a public whose one wish was to be so startled
and amused. The pleasure, however luxurious, of hearing St. Mary
Magdalene's eyes described as

> Two walking baths, two weeping motions,
> Portable and compendious oceans,

was not a poetic pleasure; and poetry, as a label for this particular
commodity, is not appropriate. [*SP*, pp. 173–74]

It may be recalled, first, that Housman's object in *The
Name and Nature of Poetry* is to define the essence of poetry,
the element without which it could not exist. This element,
as we learn elsewhere in the lecture, is "a vibration corresponding to what was felt by the writer," and we learn that
for Housman the peculiar function of poetry, its unique virtue, is "to transfuse emotion" (*SP*, p. 172). A poetry whose
object is to "startle by novelty and amuse by ingenuity" has
obviously fallen short of this virtue. We are again in the
realm of the Romantic categories of fancy and imagination,
but whereas Wordsworth, for example, would presumably
assign a poem of wit to the fancy as a kind of second-rate
production, Housman would go further in denying it the
name of poetry at all.

Housman's objection, however, is not to the nature of
metaphor but the use to which it has been put, to startle and
amuse, and in suggesting that simile and metaphor are inessential to poetry, he is saying nothing more than this: the
peculiar quality which constitutes the essence of poetry may
be found in the absence of simile and metaphor. Housman's
language, as befits the leading classical scholar of his generation, is quite precise. He means by the term *essence* that
which belongs to the very nature of a thing and which is

therefore incapable of being removed without destroying the thing itself. Metaphor, as an "accessory," is thus an object or device not essential in itself but which adds to the beauty or effectiveness of something else. Such a conception of metaphor does not appear to be entirely foreign to traditional conceptions of poetry. That is, it might well be agreed that a species of poetry, even successful poetry, could be found which depended for its success on something other than metaphor. And surely Housman is far from denying that metaphor is a legitimate device for conveying the elusive "vibration" which he considers the one essential element in genuine poetry. His own verse offers ample proof of that.

We are, however, still a great distance from the description of the function of metaphor offered by Brooks (and again I am using Brooks as a spokesman for a whole generation of critics). Brooks wishes us to see that metaphor, far from being a means to an end, is in fact both the means and the end. It is the poem. Consider this paragraph: "Most clearly of all, the metaphysical poets reveal the essentially functional character of all metaphor. We cannot remove the comparisons from their poems, as we might remove ornaments or illustrations attached to a statement, without demolishing the poems. The comparison is the poem in a structural sense."[5] Brooks then goes on to consider the "fundamental fallacy" which underlies Housman's account of the nature of metaphor, which is the fallacy of both Romantic and neo-classical concepts of figurative language: "In that account, metaphor is merely subsidiary. For 'to illustrate' is to illustrate something, and the illustration of a proposition implies that the proposition could be made without recourse to the illustration. Obviously the phrase 'to decorate' assumes for the decoration merely a subsidiary function. Housman, as we have seen, gives the show away by frankly regarding metaphor and simile as 'accessories.' "[6]

Brooks also gives the show away when he states in support of his contentions about the essential nature of metaphor that we "cannot remove the comparisons ... without demolishing the poems," for there is a fundamental fallacy here also. No one would deny his claim that to remove the metaphor is to destroy the poem, but the same point might be made about almost any device used in any successful poem. To remove the personification from Johnson's "The Vanity of Human Wishes" is to demolish the poem, yet no critic to my knowledge has argued that personification is essential to poetic statement. Brooks might just as well have argued that to remove the wheelbarrow, white chickens, and rainwater from William Carlos Williams's famous poem is to demolish the poem. It is obviously true, but it tells us nothing about the nature of poetry. The confusion lies in the ambiguity of the sort of claim Brooks is making about poetry. If he is simply talking about certain elements of some seventeenth-century and some modern poetry, he is saying something to which no one could object. But if, as is implied in several passages, he wished to enlarge this theory to include all poetry, he is on dangerous ground. The most cursory examination of the development of literary criticism gives us ample warning of the danger of basing a view of all poetry on the qualities of an era of poetry which happens to be in fashion at the moment.

Housman's statements on metaphor are, of course, partly the result of his lack of sympathy with the same generation of poets which Brooks finds so central to the tradition, and his inability to appreciate the poetry of the seventeenth century is unfortunate. Yet Brooks's tendency to base a description of the function of metaphor on the practice of these poets is simply the other side of the coin, the only difference being that Housman's position is the more guarded, the more traditional one, while Brooks asks us to revise the history of English poetry in light of his reading of selected poems.[7] The revision has now been at least partly effected, the very proof of which is the old-fashioned ring of much of Housman's criticism. We are now in a position to see New Criticism in a larger perspective and with the same result: Brooks's statements on wit and metaphor, anticipating what has become one of the prevailing tenets of modern criticism, now seem somewhat dated. And as the New Criticism begins to loosen its hold on the study of literature, we can more clearly see that the movement, as helpful as it was, did not solve all our critical problems.

It would not be necessary to dwell at such length on this issue were it not important both in clarifying Housman's statements on poetry, which are now in some disrepute, and in preparing the way for a discussion of his own practice as a poet, which has been regarded by some (including Brooks) as inconsistent with his theory. We cannot fault a poet because his sensibilities were not attuned to a generation of poets whom we now find central to an understanding of the development of British poetry. We can, however, demand consistency within his own conception of poetry and between his theory and practice as a poet. The suspicion has persisted that both Housman's poetics and his practice as a poet were the product of an "adolescent" mind, largely irrelevant to the modern temper. I believe that his theory at least was the product of an age and that we must now question seriously a system of criticism which has done the most to discredit it. Frederic Jameson has stated the issue quite succinctly in a discussion of the failings of modern approaches: We are all now in a position to judge the sterility of efforts to devise a coherent, positive, universally valid theory of literature, of attempts to work out some universal combination good for all times and places by weighing the various critical 'methods': the illusion of method has come to seem just as abstract and systematic an enterprise—in the bad sense—as the older theories of Beauty which it replaced."[8]

The reader who is familiar only with Housman's anthology pieces will no doubt sense a curious inconsistency between his seemingly disparaging remarks on metaphor and his practice as a poet. Many of the Housman poems we now think of as most successful are those which depend for much of their force on the poet's successful handling of metaphor,[9] and we are faced with the task of reconciling what seems to be a divergence between theory and practice. There is a possibility, of course, that Housman's statements on metaphor in *The Name and Nature of Poetry* were not carefully thought out and that he was not aware of the implications of his remarks. Such an answer, however, ignores the fact that Housman's view of metaphor conforms perfectly with his general theory of poetry and is stated with a precision which would deny the suspicion that it was merely an offhand remark offered for its shock value to an audience which was, in part, hostile to his account of the nature of poetry.

A more tenable explanation is to be found in the relationship which I have been pursuing between Housman's conception of metaphor and that held by most modern readers. I hesitate to drag Brooks into the argument again, but it happens that his discussions of Housman's poetry constitute a representative modern appraisal, and it is instructive to note the qualities of Housman's verse that Brooks finds praiseworthy. The Centenary Lecture[10] is, in general, an appreciative one in which Brooks is principally concerned with "those qualities that make the finest of Housman's poetry perdurable," but he is also interested in "opening up to a contemporary audience the problems which Housman faced and the characteristic failures and characteristic successes which he achieves."[11] The significance of the lecture for our purposes is, however, to be found in noting the poems which Brooks singles out for praise. They are, almost without exception, the poems which illustrate a daring use of metaphor or a witty conceit. He cites, for example, "Eight O'Clock," with its telescoping of the clock, time, and death. "The night is freezing fast" is discussed at length, especially the "daring" conceit in which the dead man "wears the turning globe," a figure which leads Brooks to praise Housman's "extravagance" and "audacity." "The Immortal Part" is lauded for its paradoxical view that "the immortal part of man is his skeleton—not the spirit, not the soul—but the most earthy, the most nearly mineral part of his body."[12] Brooks thinks "Bredon Hill" one of Housman's finest poems, and discusses at some length the poem's witty metaphor which treats a funeral as if it were a marriage. "1887" is praised for its "shocking" ironic climax. The implication of Brooks's discussion is that Housman succeeds when he allows the metaphor or the conceit of the poems to dominate, when his metaphors are most daring and paradoxical, in short, when he comes closest to writing a kind of metaphysical poetry. Brooks's statement on the conclusion of "The night is freezing fast" provides the key to his approach to Housman: "The metaphor with which the poem ends is as bizarre and witty as one of John Donne's."[13]

Housman's failures, on the other hand, are for Brooks usually failures in tone, which generally means that the poet has abandoned his daring figures and relied too much on his own voice. The result is sentimentality: "The emotion becomes mawkish and self-regarding. We feel that the poet himself has been taken in by his own sentiment, responds excessively, and expects us to respond with him in excess of what the situation calls for."[14] In "The Whole of Housman," published in 1941, Brooks is quite explicit in relating Housman's characteristic failures to his conception of wit and metaphor. He finds that Housman "distrusted the obscurity of metaphor to the point of reducing it to the clarity of abstraction," which is why his weaker poems are "flat and thin."[15] And his failure to develop his metaphors is traced directly to his theory of poetry:

Everywhere upon the body of his work is the evidence of limitations imposed upon his essential genius by a conscious aesthetic which was crippling to it. The proof of this, it seems to me, is that you cannot defend the best effects of his poetry in terms of the critical position laid down in The Name and Nature of Poetry. These effects can best be described in terms of the wit, irony, and even "conceit" which Housman consciously repudiated.[16]

It is worthwhile also to look at one of the poems Brooks sets down as a failure. The poem is short enough to quote in full:

> Could man be drunk for ever
>     With liquor, love, or fights,
> Lief should I rouse at morning
>     And lief lie down of nights.
>
> But men at whiles are sober
>     And think by fits and starts,
> And if they think, they fasten
>     Their hands upon their hearts.
>                       [Last Poems X]

It is not difficult to see, given Brooks's formalist assumptions, why he should label the poem a failure. It contains no daring figures; its metaphors are not functional in the sense that he would like them to be—that is, they do not carry the burden of the poem's meaning. The poem does not contain the kind of irony or paradox which would disguise the emotion of the speaker or render it more acceptable to a reader on his guard against sentimentality. The final dramatic gesture is, for Brooks, too theatrical and, again, sentimental. One could, I believe, demonstrate that the poem "works" as well as many of those cited by Brooks, that its theatricality is a carefully studied device, and that it is, if anything, a critique of sentimentality, but these are not the points at issue. The point is rather that Brooks's school of criticism can allow only for certain kinds of successes, and its method is frequently to revise a poet's canon in order to elevate those poems with which it can deal, chalking up the remainder as failures.

Brooks's analysis of Housman's poetry in the Centenary Lecture is, it must be admitted, quite helpful, although limited, and no one can quarrel with the more pragmatic elements of formalist criticism in so far as they lead to an emphasis on interpretation and analysis of the work of art. Yet, given the assumption of formalist theory, the self-contained nature of the work of art, should we not demand a purer mode of formalist criticism than has been generally practiced—purer in the sense that it encourages us to examine the poem on its own terms, as far as that is possible, and discourages us from coming to the poem with certain preconceptions which deaden our sensibilities to effects which the poem seeks legitimately to achieve?

It seems to me ironic that the formalists should have been caught by the very snare which they warned us all against. In one of the most influential casebooks on formalism, *Theory of Literature*, René Wellek and Austin Warren distinguish between extrinsic and intrinsic approaches to the study of literature. The extrinsic approach includes all methods of study which concern themselves with setting, environment, external causes—that is, biography, psychology, history, philosophy. They mean by the intrinsic study of literature the interpretation and analysis of the work itself, "considered as a whole system of signs, or structure of signs, serving a specific aesthetic purpose."[17] The purpose of the authors' contrast is of course to point out the limitations of extrinsic criticism and to recommend the intrinsic or formalist approach. The assumption is that extrinsic approaches never get us to the work of art itself; the intrinsic leads us to the work free of the prejudice of the Marxist, the Freudian, the biographer. That assumption, however, is misleading. What Wellek, Warren, and Brooks never seem to take into account is that the system, the methodology which the critic brings to the poem, can be as extrinsic as an obsession with biography or psychology. This is especially true if the method of analysis has been based on the characteristics of the poetry of a specific historical period. Brooks's commentary on Housman's poetry in the Centenary Lecture, as elsewhere, is one instance of a historically based criticism under the guise of an intrinsic approach.

I recognize, however, that it is impossible for a commentator to come to a body of poetry innocent of all extrinsic influence. The most that can be asked is that the critic be aware of the dangers of distorting a poet's body of work by subjecting it to arbitrary norms and values. That is, one may require that the critic admit to the necessarily subjective nature of his response, not hiding it under the disguise of a methodology. It is very well to say that the nature of the work should determine the approach to be used in analysis, but that leads us in a circle, since only through analysis can the nature of the work be established.

Having suggested some of the shortcomings of a current approach to Housman's poetry, I am not in a position to offer a new method of criticism. If anything, the somewhat rigid position of the formalists should warn us against too systematic a methodology. One of the paradoxes of modern criticism is that while our attention is supposedly being directed back to the work, we are, in reality, being asked to admire not the work so much as the brilliance of the critical method being employed on the work. In The Well Wrought Urn, Brooks sometimes gives the impression that his reconstruction of, say, "Tears, Idle Tears" is better than the poem itself, which Tennyson somehow blundered into. It is the critic, not the poet, who demands our praise for resurrecting a commonplace poem by providing a method by which it may successfully be read. Since the method works better with some kinds of poems than with others, there is always a danger that the method itself may take on an evaluative function.

At the other extreme is Housman's own method of critical commentary, which in *The Name and Nature of Poetry* amounts to his admission of being unable to account for the effects that a passage of poetry produces, as in the following instance:

In these six simple words of Milton—
         Nymphs and shepherds, dance no more—
what is it that can draw tears, as I know it can, to the eyes of more readers than one? . . . Why have the mere words the physical effect of pathos when the sense of the passage is blithe and gay? I can only say, because they are poetry, and find their way to something in man which is obscure and latent, something older than the present organisation of his nature. [SP, pp. 192–93]

A modern critic would not hesitate to suggest answers to the questions Housman raises, and he would be most uneasy at Housman's solution that the words of the passage affect us "because they are poetry." Although Housman's answer is not very helpful to a reader seeking an intellectual understanding of the poem, it does have the virtue of recognizing the enigmatic and complex character of art, and, in a curious way, it locates the center of interest in the work itself in a way that modern criticism has only pretended to do. The modern critic's approach provides answers to the questions he asks about the poem, but it has the unfortunate consequence of suggesting that his answer is somehow the poem and that the enigma has been solved. Formalist critics warn us of the heresy of paraphrase, but they are not cautious enough about the heresy of analysis.

Viewing Housman's notions about the art of poetry against the background of modern criticism, one understands better, I think, the curious position in which Housman has been placed in our generation. His treatment as an anachronism results primarily from the assurance with which twentieth-century criticism has clung to its critical dogmas. It has not been fashionable for some time to voice the kind of expressive theory of poetry which underlies Housman's poetics. But after a reign of almost forty years, formalism, while retaining its obvious value as a method of working with poems, has shed some of the luster of its more theoretical bent. A current reader of the scholarly and critical journals will seldom encounter serious discussion of the intentional fallacy, the self-sufficiency of the text, or the critic as Ideal Reader, although he will find abundant evidence of the pervasiveness of formalist methodology and terminology in the discussion of discrete works of literature. Formalism has, it seems to me, been relegated to a habit of reading, while the fashion for theory has moved on to structuralism, archetypal and myth criticism, the more sophisticated psychoanalytical approaches, and a revitalized literary history. The result is a new pluralism, as well as a tendency to treat contending theories of art with more respect.

To treat Housman's theory with respect is not, however, to argue for its validity. The whole notion of a valid, "correct" theory or approach to art is impossible to defend, and Housman's attitude in *The Name and Nature of Poetry* that he is imparting "personal opinions . . . not truths" seems to me more tenable than the more dogmatic approach which has dominated criticism for more than a generation. Housman's conception of poetry is, at the very least, coherent and worthy of closer examination. His unwillingness to subject the line from Milton's *Arcades* to the rigors of close analysis and his statement on metaphor with which we began are two manifestations of a notion which is, I believe, central to his theory and practice as a poet. It is, in essence, the idea that neither the creation nor the appreciation of poetry is an intellectual endeavor. Such an idea is so foreign to our present concepts of the genesis and criticism of art that it must be examined in more detail in the context of *The Name and Nature of Poetry*, where it is most clearly articulated.

Notes

1. *A. E. Housman: Selected Prose*, ed. John Carter (Cambridge: Cambridge University Press, 1961), p. 173. All quotations from Housman's critical and scholarly writings are from this edition, hereafter cited as *SP*. All quotations from the poetry are from *The Collected Poems of A. E. Housman* (New York: Holt, Rinehart and Winston, 1965).

2. *Modern Poetry and the Tradition* (New York: Oxford University Press, 1965), p. 38. Although I am citing the edition reissued with a new introduction in 1965, the original edition was published in 1939, only six years after Housman's *The Name and Nature of Poetry*. What may seem to us now a dead issue was more vital in the thirties and forties, when the direction of modern poetry and criticism was still very much a matter of debate. See also Gerard Reedy, S. J., "Housman's Use of Classical Convention," *Victorian Poetry* 6 (1968): 51–61, which contains a brief appraisal of Housman's relationship to the New Critics.

3. *Modern Poetry and the Tradition*, pp. 13, 38.

4. Ibid., p. 15.

5. Ibid.

6. Ibid.

7. The title of the concluding chapter of *Modern Poetry and the Tradition* is "Notes for a Revised History of English Poetry."

8. "Metacommentary," *PMLA* 86 (1971): 10.

9. I am thinking of such figures as the footrace-death parallel in "To an Athlete Dying Young," the wedding-funeral metaphor in "Bredon Hill," the monetary imagery of "One-and-Twenty," the drinking metaphor of "Terence, this is stupid stuff," the fusion of the striking of the clock and death in "Eight O'Clock," and the earth-overcoat metaphor of "The night is freezing fast."

10. "Alfred Edward Housman," *Anniversary Lectures Under the Auspices of Gertrude Clarke Whittall Poetry and Literature Fund* (Washington, D. C.: Library of Congress, 1959), pp. 39–56. The essay is reprinted in Ricks, *A. E. Housman*, and my page references are to this reprinting.

11. "Alfred Edward Housman," p. 66.

12. Ibid., p. 70.

13. Ibid., p. 68.

14. Ibid., p. 69.

15. "The Whole of Housman," *Kenyon Review* 3 (1941): 107.

16. Ibid., p. 108.

17. *Theory of Literature* (New York: Harcourt, Brace, 1949), p. 129.

# 3
# THE LIMITS OF THE INTELLECT:
*The Name and Nature of Poetry*

*The Name and Nature of Poetry,* delivered at Cambridge as the Leslie Stephen Lecture for 1933 on May 9 of that year, is admittedly a minor step (some would say setback) in the development of poetic theory. Yet it has retained its importance in the history of criticism not only because it is Housman's one comprehensive statement on the art of poetry but also because its provocative statements on the nature of poetry have aroused a great deal of controversy. Reaction to the lecture was immediate, and, curiously enough, among the first to register dissatisfaction was the lecturer himself. Housman confided to his publisher Grant Richards that he did not like the lecture. It had, he said, given him a great deal of trouble. He was overpersuaded into writing it and wrote every line against his will.[1] As for his audience, it was rumored at Cambridge that I. A. Richards left the lecture muttering, "This has put us back ten years."[2] In his review of the published lecture, Ezra Pound began by remarking that the lecture had upset many of the Cambridge critics; he went on to note the "surprising and sudden limits of [Housman's] cognizance" and to state that the "bathos, slop, ambiguity, word-twisting" were enough to "finish off" the respect he had felt for Housman.[3]

Although extreme, these reactions indicate the general dismay and hostility with which Housman's pronouncements on the art of poetry have been received. *The Name and Nature of Poetry* has now become infamous in some circles (primarily those that revolve around the critical principles of Pound, Richards, and Eliot) as a prime instance of faulty and naive criticism. Pound's review suggests one reason for such a response: "During the twenty-five years wherein my acquaintance with letters has been anything but casual and my observance of English production far from disinterested, I have barged into no single indication that Mr. Housman was aware of the world of my contemporaries."[4] The Leslie Stephen Lecture thus seemed to confirm what Housman's verse also suggested: he was hopelessly out of touch with the kind of poetry which Pound was then championing and with the kind of scientific criticism for which Richards is now well known.

Though Pound's reaction was partially justified by the overall tone of the lecture, there is a danger in dismissing too readily *The Name and Nature of Poetry* as a mere anachronism, a throwback to the criticism of Wordsworth and Arnold. It could be argued to the contrary that Housman defended a conception of poetry then completely out of fashion precisely because he was aware of the world of his contemporaries. Richard Aldington has suggested that the lecture was "a satire directed against the intellectualist school" represented by Eliot and Richards.[5] Although satire is not the proper term to describe the tone of the lecture, it now seems clear that the conception of poetry and criticism offered by Housman represented a frontal attack on the scientific criticism of Richards and his school. There can be little doubt that one of Housman's aims in the lecture was to define the limits of a systematic scientific approach and of the intellect itself in the criticism of poetry.

That Housman was aware of the critical mood of his time is evidenced by the careful distinctions he draws between science and criticism, the intellect and the emotions. His introductory apology that his role as a classical scholar did not qualify him as a literary critic and that his remarks must be taken as "personal opinions . . . not truths" (SP, p. 169) should therefore not be regarded as mere rhetoric designed to disarm his opponents. Such a view of the dichotomy of scholarship (which he regarded as a truly scientific enterprise) and criticism is consistent with the position Housman took throughout his career. In the *Introductory Lecture* delivered at University College London, in October, 1892, Housman informed his audience that "if a man wants really penetrating judgments, really illuminating criticism on a classical author, he is ill advised if he goes to a classical scholar to get them" (*SP*, p. 14). This is true because "no amount of classical learning can create a true appreciation of literature in those who lack the organs of appreciation," and conversely, "no great amount of classical learning is needed to quicken and refine the taste and judgment of those who do possess such organs" (*SP*, p. 15). Although he valued the literary critic more highly even than the classical scholar as the "rarest of all the great works of God" (*SP*, p. 158),[6] Housman never lost sight of the distinction between the aims and methods of the two enterprises of literary and textual criticism, and his distinction is significant in the approach he adopts in *The Name and Nature of Poetry*. It determines to a great extent his defense of subjectivism in literary criticism and his attack on the kind of scientifically oriented theory then in favor with Richards and the young Cambridge critics. In Housman's view, it was his own specialty, textual criticism, which was scientific in nature, literary criticism being more a matter of possessing the proper "organs of appreciation."[7] In the introduction to *The Name and Nature of Poetry*, Housman thus adopts the attitude of a "man of science" (the term is his own) discussing a subject "much less precise, and therefore less suitable to [his] capacity" as a scientist (*SP*, p. 170).

The lack of precision which impedes a scientific approach to poetry Housman attributes to two principal causes: the vagueness of the generic term *poetry*, and the difficulty of separating the poetic elements from the nonpoetic in verse. The lecture is divided fairly evenly between these two issues, as the title, which is itself quite precise, indicates. In fact, one of the ironies of the lecture and its reception is that while it has been attacked as an impressionistic and nonsystematic hodgepodge of Housman's biases and reactions to poetry, Housman himself regarded it as the rational attempt of a scientist to treat as precisely as possible a nonscientific subject. It is, however, his assumption that poetry eludes the kind of intellectual and scientific attitude that he brought to textual emendation, an assumption deeply rooted in his experience as a scholar and poet, which determines to a great degree the shape of his theory of poetry.

The opposition between intellect and emotion, central to Housman's theory, parallels exactly his scholar-critic antithesis, and it becomes clear in following his efforts to define the essential nature of poetry just why the intellect is not, in his view, the seat of aesthetic appreciation. "There is," he says, "a conception of poetry which is not fulfilled by pure language and liquid versification, with the simple and so to speak colourless pleasure which they afford, but involves the presence in them of something which moves and touches in a special and recognisable way" (*SP*, p. 172). This element, which distinguishes poetry from verse, is emotion. "And I think that to transfuse emotion—not to transmit thought but to set up in the reader's sense a vibration corresponding to what was felt by the writer—is the peculiar function of poetry" (*SP*, p. 172). Thus, poetry makes its appeal not to the intellect but to the feelings. "Meaning is of the intellect, poetry is not" (*SP*, p. 187), and the intellect may actually interfere with the aesthetic experience. Although poetry usually has an intellectual content, "it may be inadvisable to draw it out," since "perfect understanding will sometimes almost extinguish pleasure" (*SP*, p. 187).

Housman's argument for an affective as opposed to an intellectual basis for poetry involves a lengthy demonstration which includes "touchstones" (he quotes passages illustrating the "tinge of emotion" which elevates poetry above mere verse) and a historical survey that is meant to distinguish poetry from other species of writing which have somehow acquired the name of poetry without exhibiting the essential transfusion of emotion. Again he proceeds as the scientist who, having isolated an object for examination, desires to exclude all other objects which are similar yet fail to conform to his basis of classification:

The right model for imitation is that chemist who, when he encountered, or thought he had encountered, a hitherto nameless form of matter, did not purloin for it the name of something else, but invented out of his own head a name which should be proper to it. . . .

If we apply the word poetry to an object which does not resemble, either in form or content, anything which has heretofore been so called, not only are we maltreating and corrupting language, but we may be guilty of disrespect and blasphemy. Poetry may be too mean a name for the object in question: the object, being certainly something different, may possibly be something superior. [*SP*, p. 174]

It is important to notice that Housman is not making distinctions between good and bad poetry, but between poetry and something else which resembles it, although the distinction becomes somewhat blurred as he proceeds to his attack on the verse of the seventeenth and eighteenth centuries. He offers two historical examples of nonpoetry, the first being a purely intellectual verse which should properly be labeled wit:

There was a whole age of English in which the place of poetry was usurped by something very different which possessed the proper and specific name of wit: wit not in its modern sense, but as defined by Johnson, 'a combination of dissimilar images, or discovery of occult resemblances in things apparently unlike.' Such discoveries are no more poetical than anagrams; such pleasure as they give is purely intellectual and is intellectually frivolous; but this was the pleasure principally sought and found in poems by the intelligentsia of fifty years and more of the seventeenth century. [*SP*, p. 173]

Housman's guiding distinction between intellect and emotion is clearly at work here. A pleasure which is "purely intellectual" is not, in his conception, a poetic pleasure, "and poetry, as a label for this particular commodity, is not appropriate" (*SP*, p. 174).

The second instance of mere verse masquerading as poetry Housman labels "sham poetry," which he defines as "a counterfeit deliberately manufactured and offered as a substitute" (*SP*, p. 175). In England the "great historical example" of "sham poetry" is the verse produced in "the period lying between *Samson Agonistes* in 1671 and *Lyrical Ballads* in 1798" (*SP*, p. 175). Its principal exponents were Dryden and Pope. Its primary deficiency is a deficiency in feeling: "The human faculty which dominated the eighteenth century and informed its literature was the intelligence. . . . Man had ceased to live from the depths of his nature; he occupied himself for choice with thoughts which do not range beyond the sphere of the understanding" (SP, p. 176). Once again the meddling intellect is at fault, stifling the spontaneity of feeling, the transfusion of emotion without which verse forfeits its claim to the name of poetry: "To poets of the eighteenth century high and impassioned poetry did not come spontaneously, because the feelings which foster its birth were not then abundant and urgent in the inner man" (SP, p. 177).

Housman's attack on the diction of eighteenth-century verse proceeds from the same basis. It was a poverty-stricken language primarily because "it could not express human feelings with a variety and delicacy answering to their own" (SP, p. 178). Furthermore, through a circular process the limitation of language itself served to inhibit the feelings: "this deadening of language had a consequence beyond its own sphere: its effect worked inward, and deadened perception. That which could no longer be described was no longer noticed" (SP, p. 178). Housman pursues his attack on the "impure verbiage" of the eighteenth century with such zeal that he almost loses sight of his original aim of treating the name and nature of poetry. Piling up instance after instance of the false diction of Dryden and Pope, he seems to forget momentarily that his example of the "sham poetry" of the eighteenth century was offered only to demonstrate the "native ambiguity" of the term *poetry* and the difficulty of dealing with such an imprecise generic name with any degree of precision. When he returns to his subject, he is confronted with another difficulty inherent in his nonintellectual conception of poetry—how does the reader recognize poetry if he comes across it?

The first half of the lecture is devoted primarily to the name of poetry, that is, a definition of the term itself. The second half deals generally with the nature of poetry, but since, in Housman's conception, poetry is defined in terms of the presence of "something which moves and touches in a special and recognisable way," his primary emphasis is now on the percipient. Here again, Housman's aim is to deny the validity of an intellectual or scientific criticism of poetry. The problem he poses is one that is not frequently considered in literary criticism: how does one determine the competence or incompetence of the judge or critic of poetry? His answer follows logically from the conception of poetry offered in the first half of the lecture. Since the essence of poetry lies in its affective powers, the perception of poetry is determined by the "sensibility or insensibility of the percipient" (SP, p. 184). For Housman, the question "Am I capable of recognizing poetry if I come across it?" is exactly the same as "Do I possess the organ by which poetry is perceived?" (SP, p. 184). Competence in judging poetry (or distinguishing between poetry and nonpoetry) thus ultimately lies not in one's intellect, training, or aesthetics but in one's physiological makeup. The term *organ* (which Housman had used in exactly the same sense in the *Introductory Lecture* over forty years earlier) implies a purely physical reaction which excludes abstract theory or mental operations of any kind.

At this point one may perhaps feel that Housman's efforts to deny the relevance of the intellect to the appreciation of poetry has led him to an untenable position. Yet it should be kept in mind that Housman is concerned only with the question of recognizing poetry, of appreciating the distinction between poetry and something else which resembles it; he is not concerned with other critical functions such as making qualitative statements about different sorts of poetry or analyzing the techniques employed in poetry. Presumably, he would agree that there are legitimate intellectual activities connected with the criticism of poetry. He implies as much in the opening remarks of the lecture:

There is indeed one literary subject on which I think I could discourse with profit, because it is also scientific, so that a man of science can handle it without presumption, and indeed is fitter for the task than most men of letters. The Artifice of Versification, which I first thought of taking for my theme today, has underlying it a set of facts which are unknown to most of those who practise it; and their success, when they succeed, is owing to instinctive tact and a natural goodness of ear. This latent base, comprising natural laws by which all versification is conditioned, and the secret springs of the pleasure which good versification can give, is little explored by critics. [SP, p. 169]

Thus, Housman would not deny that there are functions of criticism which may be served by the intellect. It is only the most crucial area of criticism, the apprehension and appreciation of poetry, which is nonintellectual.

When such a qualification is made, Housman's conception of poetry appears less arbitrary. What his detractors have ignored is that the aim of the Leslie Stephen Lecture was quite restricted (although it was, at the same time, quite ambitious). In examining the name and nature of poetry, Housman was attempting to do no more and no less than identify the essence of poetry, the one element which separates poetry from other species of writing and without which it could not exist. Can poetry, he asks, "be isolated and studied by itself? for the combination of language with its intellectual content, its meaning, is as close a union as can well be imagined. Is there such a thing as pure unmingled poetry, poetry independent of meaning?" (SP, p. 187). The closest he comes to answering this question is in the often misunderstood comparison of Blake and Shakespeare. He finds that Blake is the most "poetical" of all poets:

I call him more poetical than Shakespeare, even though Shakespeare has so much more poetry, because poetry in him preponderates more than in Shakespeare over everything else, and instead of being confounded in a great river can be drunk pure from a slender channel of its own. Shakespeare is rich in thought, and his meaning has power of itself to move us, even if the poetry were not there: Blake's meaning is often unimportant or virtually non-existent, so that we can listen with all our hearing to his celestial tune. [SP, p. 189]

Jacob Bronowski's consideration of this passage illustrates the danger of misreading Housman's intent in the comparison of the two poets. He finds that the passage must mean one of two things: "Either Blake is the best poet, or he is not the best poet."[8] These are certainly not the only two alternatives, nor are they even relevant alternatives. Housman is not attempting to evaluate poets or to rank them; he is attempting to define what poetry is. When he says that Blake is more "poetical" than Shakespeare, he is saying only that the essential element of poetry (the transfusion of emotion) is found in a purer form in Blake than in Shakespeare ("instead of being confounded in a great river can be drunk pure from a slender channel"). Even though Shakespeare "has so much more poetry," Blake, Housman feels, serves as a perfect example of the poetic element he has been attempting to describe simply because that element is isolated in Blake, unmixed with the nonpoetic elements necessarily found in most poems.

The comparison of Blake and Shakespeare is central to an understanding of Housman's purpose in *The Name and Nature of Poetry,* and Bronowski's misinterpretation leads him to the conclusion that the majority of commentators on Housman's poetics have reached:

> There is only one way out of this. We must take the sentences to mean that Blake is the best poet. We must deny that Shakespeare and others are better poets. They may call up other awes, but Blake is the best poet. Perhaps Housman did mean this behind the blurring of "the most poetical of poets." If he did, the sentences are the *reductio ad absurdum* of his meaning. Blake is a good poet. But if we define poetry so that we prove him the best poet, we prove something which is absurd; and we must go back to change our definition.[9]

Such a conclusion can be drawn only by equating "most poetical" with "best," an equation which the context of the passage denies. A more legitimate conclusion which may be drawn from the Blake-Shakespeare comparison concerns Housman's bias toward "pure" poetry. In his conception, a typical poem is a combination of several components, only one of which is essentially "poetic": "Poems very seldom consist of poetry and nothing else; and pleasure can be derived also from their other ingredients. I am convinced that most readers, when they think that they are admiring poetry, are deceived by inability to analyse their sensations, and that they are really admiring, not the poetry of the passage before them, but something else in it, which they like better than poetry" (*SP,* p. 185). Housman's discussion of the nineteenth-century cult of Wordsworth clarifies what the other components of the poem are and exactly how they may interfere with the recognition of the "poetic." Following Arnold's treatment of Wordsworth in *Essays in Criticism: Sec-*

*ond Series,* Housman notes that the Wordsworthians praised their poet for the wrong reasons:

They were most attracted by what may be called his philosophy; they accepted his belief in the morality of the universe and the tendency of events to good; they were even willing to entertain his conception of nature as a living and sentient and benignant being, a conception as purely mythological as the Dryads and the Naiads. To that thrilling utterance which pierces the heart and brings tears to the eyes of thousands who care nothing for his opinions and beliefs they were not noticeably sensitive. [*SP,* p. 186]

Philosophy, beliefs, ideas of whatever kind, though they may be in "harmonious alliance" with the poetry, "are distinct from poetry itself" (*SP,* p. 186). They may be legitimately enjoyed by the reader, but they should not be confused with poetry, which "is not the thing said but a way of saying it" (*SP,* p. 187).

It is now easier to see why a purely physical response to poetry is a central tenet in Housman's theory. The ideas of a poem, no matter how significant, offer no clues to its "poetic" quality, since they are not essentially poetic in nature. "When I examine my mind and try to discern clearly in the matter, I cannot satisfy myself that there are any such things as poetical ideas" (*SP,* p. 186). This means, in effect, that the intellect is an untrustworthy guide to poetry; it may lead one to confuse poetry with the "wit" and "sham poetry" of the seventeenth and eighteenth centuries or to praise poems for the wrong reasons, as was the case of the Wordsworthians. Thus, the only verifiable means of identifying poetry lies in the reader's emotional response, and Housman offers a personal example of such a verification principle:

'Whosoever will save his life shall lose it, and whosoever will lose his life shall find it.' That is the most important truth which has ever been uttered, and the greatest discovery ever made in the moral world; but I do not find in it anything which I should call poetical. On the other hand, when Wisdom says in the Proverbs 'He that sinneth against me wrongeth his own soul; all they that hate me, love death,' that is to me poetry, because of the words in which the idea is clothed; and as for the seventh verse of the forty-ninth Psalm in the Book of Common Prayer, 'But no man may deliver his brother, nor make agreement unto God for him,' that is to me poetry so moving that I can hardly keep my voice steady in reading it. [SP, pp. 186–87]

Housman's reliance upon physiological response as the supreme test of poetry has been the source of most of the adverse criticism of his theory. J. P. Sullivan suggests the major objection to Housman's physical test: "Housman offers a set of physical reactions as a touchstone: that such reactions might be built up artificially by non-poetical feelings such as sentiment or familiarity he never considers. Obviously such feelings could be roused by cheap as well as good poetry."[10] It is true that physical reactions may be built up by nonpoetic feelings, but it is not true that Housman fails to consider this problem. In fact, his aim is to distinguish as precisely as possible between poetic and nonpoetic feelings aroused by the poem. In doing so, he eliminates as nonpoetic the philosophy, beliefs, sentiments, ideas of the poem—everything, that is, except the language "in which the idea is clothed." He further states that the poetic effect of language can be ascertained "by experiment" (SP, p. 187). That is, a thought produces an emotional response in the wording of the Book of Common Prayer, but "the same thought in the bible version . . . I can read without emotion" (SP, p. 187). To Sullivan's objection that feelings may be roused by cheap as well as good poetry, Housman, had he the chance to answer, might well reply that poetry is "cheap" or "good" in proportion to the ability of the poem's language to "describe natural objects with sensitive fidelity to nature" and to "express human feelings with a variety and delicacy answering to their own" (SP, p. 178). Ultimately, the ability to distinguish between good poetry and cheap poetry lies in the "sensibility or insensibility of the percipient," and the percipient's response is to the language of the poem. The reader who is sensitive to language, Housman assumes, would simply not be moved by "cheap" poetry.

Housman's conception of poetry places a great burden on the native sensibilities of the reader, and he is quick to point out that "the majority of civilised mankind notoriously and indisputably do not . . . possess the organ by which poetry is perceived" (SP, p. 184). This accounts for his view of the rarity of the true literary critic, who appears "once in a century, or once in two centuries" (SP, p. 168). Apparently, Matthew Arnold is the only nineteenth-century English critic Housman deems worthy of the title, but his praise of Arnold (in the *Introductory Lecture* of 1892) is extravagant: "When it comes to literary criticism, heap up in one scale all the literary criticism that the whole nation of professed scholars ever wrote, and drop into the other the thin green volume of Matthew Arnold's Lectures on Translating Homer which has long been out of print because the British public does not care to read it, and the first scale, as Milton says, will straight fly up and kick the beam" (SP, p. 15).

*The Name and Nature of Poetry* shows clearly the influence of Arnold's criticism, which is most readily apparent in the touchstones Housman employs throughout the lecture. Indeed, his procedure for identifying poetry parallels the system Arnold elaborated in his essay "The Study of Poetry." Housman accepted Arnold's assumption that great poetry is recognized intuitively, and he would no doubt champion Arnold's distinction between the critics' abstractions and the felt quality of the poetry itself:

Critics give themselves great labour to draw out what in the abstract constitutes the characters of a high quality of poetry. It is much better simply to have recourse to concrete examples; — to take specimens of poetry of the high, the very highest quality, and to say: The characters of a high quality of poetry are what is expressed there. They are far better recognized by being felt in the verse of the master, than by being perused in the prose of the critic.[11]

It is Arnold who gives sanction to Housman's emphasis on the validity of the feelings in apprehending the poetic. Housman notes after quoting "a typical example of poetry": "Indeed a promising young poetaster could not do better than lay up that stanza in his memory, not necessarily as a pattern to set before him, but as a touchstone to keep at his side" (SP, p. 171).

Housman also echoes Arnold in his distinctions between the poetic and the nonpoetic and in his dichotomy of science and literature. His remarks on the Wordsworthians who praise their master for the wrong reasons are paraphrased from Arnold, and his attempt to separate the sphere of the intellect from that of the emotions sounds very much like Arnold's defense of literature in "Literature and Science," which is based on the premise that science confines itself to the intellect whereas literature affects the whole man: "Interesting, indeed, these results of science are, important they are, and we should all of us be acquainted with them. But what I now wish you to mark is, that we are still, when they are propounded to us and we receive them, we are still in the sphere of intellect and knowledge."[12] Literature, on the other hand, has "an undeniable power of engaging the emotions,"[13] hence, for Arnold, its superiority as a humanistic endeavor.

Arnold's influence on Housman's conception of both poetry and criticism was undoubtedly strong. Housman regarded him not only as the greatest critic of his century but also as one of its finest poets. Yet it was Wordsworth, perhaps partly through Arnold, who exercised the most profound force on Housman's assumptions concerning the emotive nature of poetry. Housman characterized Wordsworth as "the chief figure in English poetry after Chaucer, if redemption ranks next to creation," and he suggested that "no poet later born . . . entirely escaped his influence" (SP, p. 109).[14] Housman's own poetry testifies to the accuracy of his judgment, and his account of the process by which his poetry came into being demonstrates that his conception of the nature of poetry is essentially that of Wordsworth. He devotes the concluding paragraphs of the lecture to a description of the origins of his own poetry, a description which acknowledges that his opinions on poetry are "necessarily tinged" by the experience of creating poetry:

Having drunk a pint of beer at luncheon — beer is a sedative to the brain, and my afternoons are the least intellectual portion of my life — I would go out for a walk of two or three hours. As I went along, thinking of nothing in particular, only looking at things around me and following the progress of the seasons, there would flow into my mind, with sudden and unaccountable emotion, sometimes a line or two of verse, sometimes a whole stanza at once, accompanied, not preceded, by a vague notion of the poem which they were destined to form part of. Then there would usually be a lull of an hour or so, then perhaps the spring would bubble up again. [SP, p. 194]

This sounds suspiciously like Wordsworth's "spontaneous overflow of powerful feelings," and Housman was aware of the echo, for he quotes Wordsworth's definition as evidence that "other poetry came into existence in the same way" (*SP*, pp. 193–94).

Housman's description of the origins of his poetry, however, is meant to accomplish something else. He offers it as yet another proof of the thesis that underlies the lecture: the purely emotional nature of poetry and its imperviousness to the intellect. His emphasis is on the "passive and involuntary process" (*SP*, p. 194) which brings poetry into being. His aside—"beer is a sedative to the brain, and my afternoons are the least intellectual portion of my life"—seems almost to be directed to the Cambridge critics like Richards who would make the study of poetry a science. The course of the whole lecture constitutes a rather sophisticated argument against such an approach.

It is not surprising, then, that Housman's conception of poetry and criticism should have been discredited by an era dominated by the kind of criticism he was attempting to counter. If the scientist is indeed the proper model for the literary critic, then Housman's conclusions have been correctly assessed as thoughtless and naive. But if *The Name and Nature of Poetry* is useful to modern criticism, it is precisely because it calls this assumption into question, for Housman asserts that the critic's function is in no way parallel to that of the scientist, the historian, or the sociologist.

The lecture, it is true, performs an essentially negative function, since it was, in part, a reaction to a shift in the direction of criticism at a time when science had come to dominate the mentality of an age. At the time it was delivered, it represented a holding action, as the response of Richards indicates. Now, seen in a larger perspective, it has the ring of a revolutionary document, striving to loosen the hold of science on the critical imagination.

Housman asks us to acknowledge that the essence of literature lies in a felt quality, not in a rational formulation. It is perhaps significant that his attempt to free poetry and criticism from the tyranny of the intellect has much in common with the contemporary reaction to criticism's obsession with content and interpretation, a reaction typified by Susan Sontag's essay "Against Interpretation." Like Housman, she proposes that the essentially sensuous appeal of art is restricted and enfeebled by the dominance of the intellect:

> Like the fumes of the automobile and of heavy industry which befoul the urban atmosphere, the effusion of interpretations of art today poisons our sensibilities. In a culture whose already classical dilemma is the hypertrophy of the intellect at the expense of energy and sensual capability, interpretation is the revenge of the intellect upon art.
>
> Even more, it is the revenge of the intellect upon the world. To interpret is to impoverish, to deplete the world—in order to set up a shadow world of "meanings."[15]

Interpretation, which is for Sontag an excessive stress on content and meaning, is the inevitable result of the dominance of the intellect, with its endeavor to free criticism from the subjectivity of the purely sensual response. The inherent danger of such an undertaking, however, is the loss of the sensory experience, the deadening of the sensibilities, which Housman saw as having taken place in the eighteenth century and which Sontag sees taking place in our own culture:

> Interpretation takes the sensory experience of the work of art for granted, and proceeds from there. This cannot be taken for granted, now. . . . Ours is a culture based on excess, on overproduction; the result is a steady loss of sharpness in our sensory experience. All the conditions of modern life—its material plenitude, its sheer crowdedness—conjoin to dull our sensory faculties. And it is in the light of the condition of our senses, our capacities (rather than those of another age), that the task of the critic must be assessed.[16]

Perhaps it is not too much to claim that the theory offered in *The Name and Nature of Poetry*, while it is too restricted to serve as the groundwork for any comprehensive aesthetic, deserves its small place in any reassessment of the task of the critic in our culture.

Although such a reassessment may be too distant a prospect to excite much interest, *The Name and Nature of Poetry* is also useful to us in more immediate ways. Because it has been viewed primarily as an anomaly, it has never achieved its proper role in a more modest assessment—that of Housman's own poetic art. Yet the work tells us more about the nature of Housman's poetry than may be at first apparent from its general tone.

## Notes

1. Grant Richards, *Housman, 1897–1936* (New York: Oxford University Press, 1942), pp. 275–76.

2. See Richard Aldington, *A. E. Housman and W. B. Yeats* (Hurst, Berkshire: The Peacock Press, 1955), p. 11. Another version of this incident has "one Cambridge critic" lamenting that "it would take twelve years to undo the harm Housman had done in an hour" (J. P. Sullivan, "The Leading Classic of His Generation," *Arion* 1, No. 2 [1962]: 113).

3. "Mr. Housman at Little Bethel," *Criterion* (1934): 216, 218, 222.

4. "Mr. Housman at Little Bethel," p. 217.

5. *A. E. Housman and W. B. Yeats*, p. 11.

6. This remark occurs in Housman's preface to *Nine Essays* by Arthur Platt (Cambridge: Cambridge University Press, 1927).

7. In "The Application of Thought to Textual Criticism," a paper read to the Classical Association in 1921, Housman offered this definition: "Textual criticism is a science, and, since it comprises recension and emendation, it is also an art. It is the science of discovering error in texts and the art of removing it" (*SP*, p. 131).

8. "Alfred Edward Housman," *The Poet's Defence* (Cambridge: Cambridge University Press, 1939), p. 217.

9. "Alfred Edward Housman," pp. 217–18.

10. "The Leading Classic of His Generation," p. 114.

11. "The Study of Poetry," *Essays in Criticism: Second Series*, in *Works of Matthew Arnold* 4 (London: Macmillan, 1903): 15.

12. "Literature and Science," *Discourses in America*, in *Works of Matthew Arnold*, 4:335.

13. Ibid., p. 339.

14. These remarks occur in Housman's review of volume 9 of *The Cambridge History of English Literature* in the *Cambridge Review*, January 27, 1915.

15. "Against Interpretation," *Against Interpretation and Other Essays* (New York: Farrar, Straus and Giroux, 1961), p. 7

16. Ibid., pp. 13–14.

4
# THE POETRY OF INSIGHT:
## *Persona and Point of View*

ONE INDICATION OF Housman's singular position in the tradition of British poetry at the turn of the century may be seen in his commentators' preoccupation with the nature of his verse. More perhaps than any other poet of his generation Housman has prompted questions of classification and definition in regard to a small body of poetry which does not fit easily into any school or movement. For the critics of the thirties, it was primarily a question of classicism versus romanticism, a debate which reached its height in a series of letters in the *New Statesman and Nation* in 1936 and which has been intermittently revived.[1] Yet despite numerous subsequent efforts to articulate the special character of Housman's verse, one must agree with Christopher Ricks's observation that we are still "hard put to say why we like or dislike his poems."[2] It is the very nature of his poetry which remains in question.

Housman, as we know from his statements in *The Name and Nature of Poetry,* had little sympathy with the efforts of criticism to label and define what was for him a personal and human response, and there is something to be said for his concern that the tendency of criticism in his time was to confuse the provinces of literature and science. But he was obviously not opposed to the more humanistic branch of literary criticism, typified in the nineteenth century by his favorite critic Matthew Arnold, and his primary objection to twentieth-century criticism was centered on its attempt to substitute empirical truth for informed opinion and good taste. Housman's cautious position on the limits of the intellect in the appraisal of poetry voiced in *The Name and Nature of Poetry* should serve to remind the commentator how tentative and even capricious his own pronouncements may be, and the tone of tentative inquiry befitting an admirer of Housman and Arnold is the tone I wish to take here.

Two attempts to define the poetic quality of Housman's verse, those of Christopher Ricks and F. W. Bateson, have been somewhat more ambitious, but although the title of Ricks's essay, "The Nature of Housman's Poetry," has the ring of a definitive statement, its method is more modest, and one quickly sees that Ricks is not exactly defining the nature of Housman's poetry but isolating one of its most characteristic effects: "To me his poems are remarkable for the ways in which rhythm and style temper or mitigate or criticise what in bald paraphrase the poem would be saying."[3] Ricks finds that in some of Housman's finest poems *what is said* is at odds with *how* it is said, producing contrarieties and disparities of feeling which complicate what would otherwise appear to be simple and even sentimental poems. His discussion of this effect, although limited, is convincing, and the essay is perhaps the most helpful and suggestive analysis of Housman's style we have had.

Bateson also locates the definitive quality of Housman's poetry in a union of contrarieties:

> The critical problem . . . that is posed by Housman's best poems is the apparent union of two apparently incompatible qualities—a classic concision of style and a romantic extremism of temperament. I stress the *appearance* of both the union and the incompatibility, because, the reality which lies behind the appearance is, I believe, neither strictly classical nor romantic. I shall call it *emphasis*, a stylistic quality that is inherent in Latin and difficult to attain in English without the artificial aids of italics or capital letters.[4]

The poetry of emphasis, as Bateson labels Housman's verse, is an English parallel to the Roman lyric and uses the emphatic elements of English—the monosyllable, internal rhyme and the compound word—in a manner similar to the Latin use of the elaborate system of case endings; moods, tenses, and persons of the verb; and grammatical genders to achieve brevity and concentration. Bateson's notion that Housman's verse exhibits a fusion of classical style and romantic temperament has become something of a critical commonplace and was, in fact, one of the issues of debate in the controversy carried on in the *New Statesman and Nation*. He is also hard put to demonstrate his new designation of emphasis, but his description is helpful, especially as it offers an explanation for the peculiar sense of concentration one feels in Housman's verse not ordinarily found in a romantic poet.

The descriptions of Ricks and Bateson, taken together, come closer to defining the felt quality of Housman's verse than anything we have been offered before, and Bateson is correct, I think, in stating that it is a quality "almost unprecedented in English poetry."[5] Although they pursue different routes, both arrive at the same end—the conflict between the temperament of the poem's speaker and the style of the poem as a whole. Here, I believe, is the beginning point for any investigation of the nature of Housman's poetry, but the conflict between speaker and poem must be seen in a larger context which includes the dramatic situation Housman created for virtually all of his poetry, the character he chose for his poetic mask, and the theory of poetry which led both to the naiveté of his poetic voice and the oft-remarked "purity" of his poetic style.

The problem of the relationship between Housman's theory of poetry and his own practice as a poet is, however, a knotty one. Ricks uses *The Name and Nature of Poetry* to support his contention that "contrarieties and disparities of feeling" constitute the best part of Housman's verse, but most commentators have seen the theory as providing a negative influence on the poetry. Cleanth Brooks, in a statement I referred to in chapter 2, offers us a picture of a natural genius hamstrung by a wrong headed theory of art:

Everywhere upon the body of his work is the evidence of limitations imposed upon his essential genius by a conscious aesthetic which was crippling to it. The very proof of this, it seems to me, is that you cannot defend the best effects of poetry in terms of the critical position laid down in *The Name and Nature of Poetry*. Those effects can best be described in terms of the wit, irony and even "conceit," which Housman consciously repudiated. . . . Some of the poems that Housman wrote are very good indeed. But the best of his poetry seems to me poetry achieved in spite of the immediate tradition out of which he wrote.[6]

Brooks's view is colored by his own antipathy to that tradition, and the effects which he admires in Housman are not necessarily those which are characteristic of his poetry but those effects which Brooks looks for and finds throughout the tradition of British and American poetry.

The theory articulated in *The Name and Nature of Poetry* can provide some help for an approach to Housman's verse if we do not allow it to take us too far. At the very least it can give us some sense of Housman's conception of the tradition out of which he was writing. That tradition, as Housman defined it, suggests that we should expect to encounter a poetry of feeling in the manner of the Romantics, although not necessarily in the Romantic style. It suggests further that we should not expect to find anything approaching the formulation of a philosophical world view or the exposition of ideas, since Housman was convinced that his verse made its appeal not to the intellect but "to something in man which is obscure and latent, something older than the present organisation of his nature . . ." (*SP*, p. 172).

We have seen that the opposition between intellect and emotion is central to Housman's concept of poetry, and that in his effort to define the essential nature of poetry he took great pains to show that the intellect is not the seat of appreciation. He was also careful to distinguish between meaning, a function of the intellect, and the essential aesthetic experience, a product of the emotions: "Meaning is of the intellect, poetry is not" (*SP*, p. 187). Although poetry usually has an intellectual content, "it may be inadvisable to draw it out," since "perfect understanding will sometimes almost extinguish pleasure" (*SP*, p. 187). *The Name and Nature of Poetry* thus reinforces what a reading of the collected poems makes clear: considered both thematically and technically, Housman's poetry constitutes what might well be called a poetry of insight, if we understand by that term a poetry which is concerned primarily with the speaker's obscure, intuitive, almost preintellectual sense of his human situation. Although almost all lyric poetry might be called in some sense a poetry of insight, the term has special relevance to Housman's verse since it locates the center of interest in the point of view assumed by his created persona.

I am convinced that Housman's commentators have gone astray in pursuing the philosophy of his poetry, just as Housman believed Wordsworth's admirers were misdirected in concentrating on his philosophy of nature. In both cases we are confronted with a sense of the world which is beyond (or below) the intellect. That is, the poetry does not lend itself readily to philosophical schema or systemization. Further, Housman's poems are frequently concerned with nothing more than dramatizing the moment in which insight occurs. It is a commonplace of Housman criticism that he kept writing the same poem, and that poem most frequently is a means of placing the persona in a situation in which some vague sense of his condition is realized. The structures, the strategies of the poems, moreover, serve most often to convey the shock of recognition, the moment of insight.

The most obvious of Housman's strategies is the creation of a rustic persona—the Shropshire lad of the first volume—who controls the tone of almost the entire body of his verse with the few exceptions in which the narrator is ill-defined or unimportant as a distinct voice. John Stevenson has examined both Housman's motives for this device and the character he has created in his perceptive essay "The Martyr as Innocent: Housman's Lonely Lad." His analysis indicates the value of an essentially naive speaker in dramatizing the characteristic movement from innocence to experience: "The lad is variously the soldier, the lover, the 'young sinner,' and the rustic observer or commentator on life. In any of the roles, he is almost invariably characterized by his ingenuousness in the grip of a strong emotion, by what is often defined as on the threshold of discovery. He is awkward, but straightforward in his actions, and always the process of discovery results in a revelation of some kind."[7] Reading in the collected poems, one is struck not only with the frequency with which this revelatory moment is treated but also with the variety of effects Housman achieves with his rustic persona.

One may also note in examining the best known of Housman's poems the types of situations in which Housman involves his persona. A celebration of the fifty years that God has saved the queen serves to remind him of the soldiers buried in foreign fields who shared the work with God, giving him a momentary glimpse of the mortality on which the permanence of the race is founded. A walk through the woods at Eastertide to observe the cherry in bloom produces a sudden intimation of mortality. The lad at two-and-twenty exclaims, of the transience of love, "And oh, 'tis true, 'tis true." A storm on Wenlock Edge, the site of an ancient Roman city, leads to the knowledge that "Then 'twas the Roman, now 'tis I." An athlete dying young, a funeral observed from Bredon Hill, the sounds of the soldiers' tread, the imagined last hour of a murderer who hangs at the stroke of eight—these are the occasions for the innocent's confrontation with the alien world of time and death.

But it is the manner in which Housman conveys to us the significance of the discovery that provides the force of many of his best poems. At times the poem depends on the paradox or irony of poems like "To an Athlete Dying Young" or "1887," so much admired by the New Critics. Yet he may also employ more subtle means in which no daring metaphors or metaphysical conceits are evident. Consider, for example, one of the most straightforward of the poems of *A Shropshire Lad*, "Loveliest of Trees," which has been generally admired. The tone of the poem clearly depends on the point of view of the naive persona, his essential innocence, and even his inability to articulate with any sophistication what he has discovered. His attitude is difficult to characterize, for it is not governed by pessimism or bitterness at his human state. Housman seems interested primarily in the persona's discovery of his own mortality, and the poem is structured in such a manner as to make that discovery its central element. The poem depends to a great extent on a curious but obscure relationship between the sight of the cherry in bloom at Eastertide and a sense of human limitation. The first stanza concentrates wholly on the description of the cherry, "wearing white for Eastertide," and the second stanza on the persona's realization of his mortality. The

causal connection between the two experiences is left un-
stated. Perhaps it is not capable of discursive statement. The
lad's calculation of his threescore years and ten is handled in
an almost neutral manner, with no betrayal of emotion:

> Now, of my threescore years and ten,
> Twenty will not come again,
> And take from seventy springs a score,
> It only leaves me fifty more.

There is more attention to arithmetic than to feeling here,
much in the manner of Frost's "Stopping by Woods on a
Snowy Evening," where the persona seems more involved
with the owner of the woods and the horse than with the
consequences of his experience. But in both cases the effect
is the same. John Ciardi has spoken of the duplicity of Frost's
method, and the term is applicable here. In both cases, the
force of the poem is greater than the occasion or the accumu-
lation of details would seem to warrant. The opposite effect
is sentimentality, a constant threat for poets like Frost and
Housman who deal in potentially melodramatic situations.

The understatement of the last stanza provides an instance
of Housman's characteristic treatment of the consequences
of insight:

> And since to look at things in bloom
> Fifty springs are little room,
> About the woodlands I will go
> To see the cherry hung with snow.

The details of the stanza carry a significance hardly warranted by the commonplace sentiment they express or the
simple language in which they are couched, and that results
almost entirely from the fact that they are now weighted by
the persona's intuitive sense of his own mortality. "Things
in bloom" now suggest something of the vitality of life
which has become more precious. The limitation of life is
carried by the understatement of "little room," and the sense
of death which now colors all living things is conveyed by
the single description of the white blossoms of the cherry,
"hung with snow." It is an effect which relies on what is
unsaid, comparable to the similar conclusion of Frost's
poem, "And miles to go before I sleep," although Frost's line

seems almost heavy-handed in comparison. The poem also relies on its progressive structure and on its pattern of imagery, both of which warrant further discussion, but at the moment I should like to pursue the thematics of a poetry of insight, especially as it involves the problems of character and point of view.

It would be misleading to state that the point of view adopted by the persona in "Loveliest of Trees" is typical of that of the majority of Housman's poems. His reaction to the discoveries he makes in poem after poem varies from renewed vitality to melancholy. What remains constant is, however, the degree to which the poems depend for their effect on the character of the persona, his ability to voice afresh sentiments which in the mouth of a more sophisticated speaker would appear trite. Housman avoids the dangers of the trite, the sentimental by separating himself from his poems through a created character, while a poet like Frost pretends actually to be the homely rustic speaker that the poem demands, a role Frost apparently found congenial to his public life as a poet. Housman's poetics are not elaborate enough to allow for Yeats's theory of the mask, but the result of the split between poet and persona produces a similar situation. His solution to the problems of personality and persona which Yeats spent a lifetime working out was simply to create the fiction of the Shropshire lad, substituting for the voice of the learned classical scholar, whose reticence was almost legendary, that of the rustic innocent, who declares

> Some can gaze and not be sick,
> But I could never learn the trick.
> There's this to say for blood and breath,
> They give a man a taste for death.
> [*Additional Poems* XVI]

The persona thus becomes a kind of Yeatsian mask or anti-self, the opposite of all that the poet represents in his private life.[8] The resulting tone, carefully cultivated, controls Housman's verse so pervasively that it becomes easy to blur the distinction between the personalities of poet and speaker, as is evidenced by the greater part of available criticism on Housman's verse.

The nature of the persona we may expect to encounter in Housman's verse—initially the innocent confronted with the alien world, later the exile seeking to recapture his lost innocence—has been described in some detail. I should like to examine another aspect of the persona, the effect of his presence in the poems as a whole. That is, what does Housman gain or lose by the device of the pastoral mask? It is a question which can be answered only by examination of specific poems, for his presence is felt more strongly in some poems than in others. Housman rarely drops the mask, but sometimes it is crucial, at other times it seems only a habit of composition.

To look first at an instance in which the character and point of view of the speaker are decisive in determining the form of the poem, we may consider Lyric XXX of *A Shropshire Lad*, "Others, I am not the first." The poem has received little attention; it contains none of the obvious designs of irony or metaphor which would attract the notice of the formalists, and I suspect it would be set down as a relative failure by many, for its tone approaches that of "Could man be drunk for ever," a poem Cleanth Brooks condemns for its theatrical gestures and sentimentality.[9] There is a kind of theatricality in "Others, I am not the first," but one must be cautious in ascribing it to the poem as a whole, as opposed to its persona, who is presented as a young man dealing with his first taste of the desire and guilt which are the fruits of experience. His attempt to order his feelings and to relieve their intensity comprises the strategy of the poem:

> Others, I am not the first,
> Have willed more mischief than they durst:
> If in the breathless night I too
> Shiver now, 'tis nothing new.
>
> More than I, if truth were told,
> Have stood and sweated hot and cold,
> And through their reins in ice and fire
> Fear contended with desire.
>
> Agued once like me were they,
> But I like them shall win my way

Lastly to the bed of mould
Where there's neither heat nor cold.
                    [ll. 1–12]

The theme of private versus shared experience achieves a
curious effect in the poem, for the speaker's determination to
console himself with the knowledge that his feelings have
been shared by other men serves only to reinforce the sense
of their privacy. In the same way, the mental process, the
argument of the poem, is continually undermined by its
physical details. The fear and desire which contend in the
reins, the seat of the passions, are ultimately stronger than
the intellect, and they render the poem's argument ineffec-
tual. It is an argument that cuts both ways: the attempt to
escape the consequences of experience leads to the further
revelation that such experience is the inescapable lot of the
condition of man.

The poem is not quite as simple as it appears in paraphrase, but some measure of its complexity can be maintained only through the separation of persona and poet. The
persona's response to his situation is obviously inadequate,
as he casts about for ways to find release from his strong
feelings. He reasons that he is no different from other men;
he tries to take comfort in the thought that men die. But the
poem as a whole, the poet's response to the experience, contrives to undermine the persona's strategy, as the poem reveals the weakness of his rationalizations by its concentration on the physical symptoms of his fear and desire. The
poem reveals the inadequacy of the intellect, the domination
of the feelings, and the conventional response of commentators to poems such as this—that Housman is advocating
death as a release from the pain of life—misses the point for
the very reason that it blurs the distinction between the poet
and speaker.

To label Housman's point of view adolescent, as has frequently been done, is to assume that he shares the innocence
of the persona, but the effect of many poems depends on the
exposure of such naiveté. "Is my team ploughing," for
example, is constructed on the contrast between the knowledge, shared by the reader and poet, that life is transient, and
the innocence maintained by a young man who has died

believing that his girl and his best friend remain unchanged:

> 'Is my girl happy,
>     That I thought hard to leave,
> And has she tired of weeping
>     As she lies down at eve?'
>
> Ay, she lies down lightly,
>     She lies not down to weep:
> Your girl is well contented,
>     Be still, my lad, and sleep.
>
> 'Is my friend hearty,
>     Now I am thin and pine,
> And has he found to sleep in
>     A better bed than mine?'
>
> Yes, lad, I lie easy,
>     I lie as lads would choose,
> I cheer a dead man's sweetheart;
>     Never ask me whose.
>         [ll. 17–32]

There is, of course, no possibility of confusion here between the two points of view, since Housman has the youth speaking from the grave, but in poems such as "The Recruit" and "Oh see how thick the goldcup flowers" the point is made in less obvious ways. In "The Recruit" the sentiments of the persona are denied by the poem itself. He assures a young soldier that he will be long remembered in his home shire, while the poem as a whole suggests the opposite.[10] In "Oh see how thick the goldcup flowers" the naiveté of the speaker is exploited in a seduction scene in which his expectations are dashed and his argument is turned against him.

There are, in fact, a great number of verses in Housman's collected poems which, because of the situations described, preclude an identification of poet and speaker, such as the following from More Poems:

> My dreams are of a field afar
>     And blood and smoke and shot.
> There in their graves my comrades are,
>     In my grave I am not.

I too was taught the trade of man
And spelt the lesson plain;
But they, when I forgot and ran,
Remembered and remain.
[XXXIX]

Whatever success the poem achieves obviously depends on the fictional background of the speaker's cowardice, his complicated attitude of regret and envy for his dead comrades, and all the trappings of war which provide the framework of the poem and which are clearly foreign to the classical scholar who wrote it. I would suggest that what is obvious here is operating in more complex ways in other poems. No matter what Housman's private compulsions for writing from the point of view of soldiers, murderers, dead men, and rustics, the use of such a point of view is a fact of his poetry, and it must be taken into account. If we examine not the personal basis for Housman's narrative devices but the results they achieve in the poetry, we are in a better position to understand his art. The poet's own emotional life, however fascinating, is at present beyond the reach of criticism.

It is clear that Housman uses his lyrics to explore the obscure and unnamed feelings which give man a sense of his human state and that he treats the feelings as somehow prior to the intellect. The theme of *The Name and Nature of Poetry*—that poetry is not of the intellect and that the intellect may hinder its production and retard its appreciation—whatever its value as a statement about art, is certainly a clue to Housman's method as an artist. It offers one explanation for his attraction to the sort of rustic persona who can express his passions without being able to account for them and whose efforts to rationalize his situation are pitiably inadequate. In *The Name and Nature of Poetry* Housman reserves his greatest praise for William Blake, "the most poetical of all poets" (SP, p. 189); and the *Songs of Innocence and of Experience* is perhaps the closest prototype for Housman's own verse, although he chooses the adolescent rather than the child for his spokesman.

What Housman gains in his use of the fiction of the Shropshire lad may be further noted in observing that many of the most admired effects of his poems—the daring conceits, the paradoxes—are merely extensions of the point of view created through the innocent persona. To select one example, "The night is freezing fast" (*Last Poems* XX) has been praised for its brilliant use of metaphor and handling of tone. Both may be traced to the speaker Housman has created for the occasion of the poem. It is the speaker's memory of his dead friend and the schoolboy attitude he adopts[11] which dictate the tone of the poem:

> The night is freezing fast,
> To-morrow comes December;
> And winterfalls of old
> Are with me from the past;
> And chiefly I remember
> How Dick would hate the cold.
>
> Fall, winter, fall; for he,
> Prompt hand and headpiece clever,
> Has woven a winter robe,
> And made of earth and sea
> His overcoat for ever,
> And wears the turning globe.

One is reminded here of Wordsworth's "A Slumber Did My Spirit Seal" with its similar images of Lucy "Rolled round in earth's diurnal course, / With rocks, and stones, and trees." There is, however, one crucial difference. Wordsworth's persona views Lucy's return to nature as a tragic loss: "No motion has she now, no force; / She neither hears nor sees." He is the bereaved lover whose love had blinded him to Lucy's earthly nature: "She seemed a thing that could not feel / The touch of earthly years." The final image of his beloved helplessly spun by the forces of the earth reinforces his sudden recognition of the reality of death which his illusion of love's permanence had denied him. Housman's young speaker, on the other hand, seems incapable of that sort of recognition. He views Dick's death as a clever strategy for outwitting the cold. Rather than becoming the helpless victim of the impersonal turning globe, Dick is seen as triumphing over the misery of life. He has at

last escaped the cold by making the earth his "overcoat for
ever." In spite of the jesting tone, or perhaps because of it,
the speaker's attitude toward death is essentially naive. It
might be compared to that taken by Wordsworth's persona
before he awoke to death's finality. Housman's speaker sees
death only in terms of life. It is as if Dick, like Lucy, could
not feel the touch of death. He attributes to Dick a will and a
purpose which are obviously based on the memory of his
personality when he was still alive: "Prompt hand and
headpiece clever." Dick was a clever man, and his wit has
finally paid off. In contrast to Wordsworth's persona, the
speaker of "The night is freezing fast" displays no sense of
the loss involved in death, but it is important to note that the
poem, as opposed to the persona, does suggest such a loss.
As Brooks notes, the gay tone "actually renders the sense of
grief not less but more intense."[12] He attributes this result to
the fact that the tone is characteristic of the dead youth, and
that may be a part of it. But what is more important in ac-
counting for the paradoxical effect the poem achieves is the
split between the persona's attitude and the attitude of the
poem as a whole. The insufficiency of the persona's view of
death is revealed in the same manner that the rhetoric of the
funeral sermon is negated by the motionless corpse. We receive a sense of what death entails in a way that the speaker
cannot. It is a curious and complex device, since it involves
the assertion of two contradictory attitudes—gaiety and
grief, triumph and defeat. The poem reveals perfectly how
nondiscursive elements may deny what, discursively, the
persona asserts.

Housman achieves this effect in a number of poems about
death. Although the "philosophy" of death in "To an
Athlete Dying Young" has been discussed as an instance of
Housman's perversity, no commentator, to my knowledge,
has sufficiently emphasized that the attitude toward death
taken in the poem is that of one of the dead athlete's friends,
not that of the poet. Housman characterizes the speaker of
the poem in several ways. In the first two stanzas he is pictured as one of the townsmen who has cheered the athlete to
victory and who now, as one close to the dead youth, bears
the coffin to the grave:

> The time you won your town the race
> We chaired you through the market-place;
> Man and boy stood cheering by,
> And home we brought you shoulder-high.
>
> To-day, the road all runners come,
> Shoulder-high we bring you home,
> And set you at your threshold down,
> Townsman of a stiller town.
>
> [ll. 1–8]

The poem is thus a kind of graveside oration delivered by one of the lads who, presumably, "wore [his] honours out":

> Now you will not swell the rout
> Of lads that wore their honours out,
> Runners whom renown outran
> And the name died before the man.
>
> [ll. 17–20]

Obviously, the speaker is acutely conscious of the transience of the "fields where glory does not stay," and one may assume that his sentiments are partly dictated by the difference he observes between the youth who died in his prime and himself. He is also characterized by the kind of schoolboy attitude seen in "The night is freezing fast." The expression "smart lad" which begins line 9 strikes me as typical of the kind of congratulatory phrase carried over from the playing fields, and it emphasizes the persona's rather commonplace analogy between life and a footrace.

Of course, the entire oration develops the conceit that death is the final victory, "the road all runners come," offering a sense of permanence which man is denied in life. Yet the relationship between what the speaker asserts and what the poem conveys is remarkably close to that of "The night is freezing fast." The persona emphasizes in his graveside address the permanence achieved by the athlete, but the total effect of the poem is to reinforce a sense of transience, of the inescapable nature of change and death. The point I would stress is that the conceit of the poem, as in "The night is freezing fast," is developed from the character of the persona, his imagined relationship to the dead man, and the occasion of the poem. To equate his point of view with that of Housman is to confuse a technique by which the poet conveys a complex reaction to death with a philosophy, an abstract idea which has no meaning outside the poem.

Instances of this kind of tension between the persona's point of view and that suggested by the poem as a whole may be found throughout Housman's poetry, although it is clearly not the only effect he achieves with his fictional speaker. It is similar to the quality that Christopher Ricks has articulated, the disparity between what is said and how it is said, although Ricks looks primarily at how rhythm and style negate or temper what the poem would be saying in paraphrase. I am suggesting that the same sort of conflict extends to what is said once we recognize the division between the speaker of the poem and the poet who, in many cases, is exploiting the naiveté of his speaker. Ricks has analyzed the passages from other poets Housman quotes in *The Name and Nature of Poetry* to support his contention that disparities of feeling fascinated the poet, and he presents a convincing argument that Housman was attracted to a kind of poetry in which the feeling is strangely at odds with what is being asserted.

It seems clear that Housman achieved much the same result from his use of the mask of the rustic. The tension between the innocence of the persona and the sophistication of the poet is evident in many of his most successful poems. It is, however, a difficult tension to sustain, and Housman is not always successful with it. When he fails, the resulting tone gives the impression that it is the poet himself whose attitude is hopelessly childish and inadequate, and it is true that in some instances Housman found his poetic mask too congenial, so that he was unable to separate himself sufficiently from the Shropshire lad. Since his persona was, in Housman's words, "an imaginary figure, with something of my temperament and view of life,"[13] it was perhaps too easy to blur the distinction. It might be argued that the statement just quoted gives evidence that there was no distinction, but that is to confuse life and art, ideas with their artistic expression. Housman stated in *The Name and Nature of Poetry* that "poetry is not the thing said but a way of saying it" (*SP*, p.

187). Although we may have all shared, at times, the emotions expressed by Housman's persona, we would not ordinarily express them in the manner in which they are expressed by the rustic, and if we did create an "imaginary figure" to give vent to our emotions, we would no longer simply be expressing feeling but creating a fiction which would necessarily modify that feeling.

Readers who object to the "philosophy" of Housman's poetry are, in reality, objecting to the mode in which a point of view toward life is being expressed, and they fail to take into account the narrative technique which Housman first employed for the poems of *A Shropshire Lad* and which carried over into the whole body of his poetry. To state the case in the most direct manner, if the feelings expressed in Housman's poetry seem adolescent to some, that is precisely because they are placed in the mouth of an adolescent. To insist on this point is not, however, to justify fully Housman's device of employing the rustic as his speaker. While it is the means by which he achieved his characteristic successes, it also imposes a severe limitation on his poetry. It is primarily responsible for the limited range of his verse and its sameness of tone. What is missing in Housman is the range of voices and attitudes that we find in a poet like Yeats, and Yeats's status as a major poet owes a great deal to the fact that he was able to overcome, through his own self-criticism and through the system constructed about his theories of self and mask, the complex problems involved in the relationship between poet and persona.

Housman seems to have been uninterested in exploring such critical problems. His convictions about poetry and criticism precluded the sort of intellectual systems as well as the tendency toward self-analysis exhibited by Yeats. He subscribed to the Romantic notion that the peculiar function of poetry was "to transfuse emotion—not to transmit thought but to set up in the reader's sense a vibration corresponding to what was felt by the writer" (*SP*, p. 172). Holding such a belief, he was naturally drawn to devices and techniques which would enable him to deal with the deepest and most elementary human feelings, and his choice of the innocent as persona allowed him to explore a range of feelings revolving around man's first discovery of the world in which he finds himself. He owes much of his success as a poet to the manner in which he was able to exploit the relationship between poet and persona, but his status as a minor poet results also in some measure from the restrictions imposed on his poetry by the nature of his persona. His stature has also been influenced by a confusion which has existed between the technique by which Housman recreated the point of view of the innocent and an alleged philosophy attributed to the poet himself.

## Notes

1. Cyril Connolly's attack on Housman was answered by F. L. Lucas, Martin Cooper, L. P. Wilkinson, and John Sparrow, Connolly getting in the last word in a final letter in the issue of June 6. Connolly reprints the controversy in *The Condemned Playground* (London: Routledge, 1945), pp. 47–62. It is also reprinted in *A. E. Housman*, ed. Christopher Ricks, pp. 35–50. For a more recent discussion of the classicism-romanticism debate see Reedy, "Housman's Use of Classical Convention," pp. 51–61.

2. "The Nature of Housman's Poetry," in *A. E. Housman*, ed. Christopher Ricks, p. 106.

3. Ibid.

4. "The Poetry of Emphasis," in *A. E. Housman*, ed. Christopher Ricks, pp. 134–35.

5. Ibid., p. 131.

6. "The Whole of Housman," p. 108.

7. *South Atlantic Quarterly* 57 (1958): 77.

8. See John Stevenson, "The Ceremony of Housman's Style," *Victorian Poetry* 10 (1972): 44–55. "He stands aside and lets the style become the mask by which he celebrates the ceremony of man's condition—the blight man was born for. Hence, the Shropshire setting, the rustic lad, the striving for the colloquial tone: the Kennedy Professor of Latin knew nothing of these country parts; he uses the setting to extinguish his personality in order to achieve the bardic tone of anonymity, to recapture what Mr. Richard Ellmann, writing of Yeats's style, describes as the 'traditionally authoritative manner of the poet.' The bardic position is always public (the ceremonial voice), and this stance is what Housman strives for in his

poetry in order to hold in tension the double view of both innocence and experience" (p. 47).

9. See "Alfred Edward Housman," in *A. E. Housman*, ed. Christopher Ricks, pp. 65–66.

10. See "Housman's 'The Recruit,' " *Explicator* 25 (1965–66),
Item 25.

11. As Cleanth Brooks notes; see "Alfred Edward Housman," pp.
68–69.

12. Ibid., p. 69.

13. See *The Letters of A. E. Housman*, p. 328.

# 5

# SONGS OF INNOCENCE AND EXPERIENCE: *Two Structural Patterns*

A PREOCCUPATION with the awakening of the consciousness to the "foreign laws of God and Man" is reflected not only in the choice of persona and the point of view but also in the structural principles Housman employs in his poems. These elements are, however, easy to overlook for the very reason that the poem gives the appearance of utter ingenuousness, an aspect of Housman's poetry which has influenced the view that he was not concerned with the formal elements of his art. The scholar who has published most widely on Housman has remarked:

Such problems as order and climax, the building up of tonal effects, nuance, and resolution did not present themselves significantly to Housman. These things came to him easily if they came at all, a part of the largesse of the afternoon's walk. When brain had to settle down to the task of putting the stanzas of a poem in order, trouble usually arose. On a larger scale, in his gathering of the sixty-three poems of his first book, it would have been contrary to Housman's nature to concern himself with any but the elementary matters of arrangement and grouping of his lyrics.[1]

The unfortunate impression given by such a view is that Housman was not bothered by the usual concerns of the artist; the poems appeared in his head spontaneously on his afternoon walks, and it was against his nature to involve himself with the niceties of form. That is perhaps the impression Housman attempted to impart with the account of the composition of his poems given in *The Name and Nature of Poetry*, essentially a restatement of Wordsworth's conception of poetry as a spontaneous overflow of powerful feelings.

It is consistent with Housman's poetics that he should have adopted one of the strongest conventions of Romanticism, the notion of spontaneity, but if we distinguish between the original impetus of the poem and the finished product, the manuscript revisions in the notebooks do not provide much evidence to support the idea. On the contrary, they show the reworking of false starts, the reorganization of stanzas, the search for the right image or sound. The revisions reveal, in fact, what one would expect from reading the neatly chiseled poems—that Housman was a fastidious artist who knew his craft well and practiced it with exactness.[2]

I have attempted to demonstrate in an earlier study that the structure of *A Shropshire Lad* as a whole reinforces the theme of the persona's movement from innocence to experience; that the ordering of the poems is deliberate and meaningful; and that Housman was indeed concerned with such problems as order and climax, the building up of tonal effects, nuance, and resolution.[3] It seems clear that his regard for these structural elements is also exhibited by the individual poems, but the myth of the naive artist is difficult to counter, especially since Housman was, in part, responsible for it through his own statements on poetry. However, some notion of Housman's attention to the structural elements of his verse can be gained by an examination of selected lyrics chosen primarily from *A Shropshire Lad* and *Last Poems*. The two collections published by Laurence Housman after his brother's death, *More Poems* and *Additional Poems*, are less rewarding, although *More Poems* contains a number of interesting lyrics. It must be recalled that these collections were not prepared for publication by the poet, and many of the verses are obviously no more than rough drafts. Nine of them are made up of only one quatrain each, a circumstance which does not occur in either of the collections Housman himself published.

Of the Housman poems which still reward study, two patterns of development occur more frequently than any other, and both are related to the theme of insight or discovery discussed in the preceding chapter. A large number of the poems of *A Shropshire Lad* deal directly with the moment of insight and exhibit a progressive structure which carries the persona from innocence to knowledge or from expectation to disillusionment. Most of these are found in the first half of *A Shropshire Lad*, which concentrates on the innocent's encounter with the alien world of death and change. In the last half of *A Shropshire Lad*, in *Last Poems*, and to some extent in the posthumous collections are found the lyrics which depend for their effect on the persona's recognition of the gulf which lies between innocence and experience and on his reaction to his exiled state. The structural patterns here are more varied because the feelings of the persona have acquired an ambivalence missing in the poems of the first group.

The progressive structure of the early *Shropshire Lad* poems depends heavily on the character of the persona elaborated in the preceding chapter. In fact, "Loveliest of Trees," discussed earlier in terms of the role of the persona, gives one of the clearest examples of the manner in which Housman is able to reveal the sense of the persona's discovery through the structure of the poem, in this case the pattern of imagery connected with the blossoming cherry. In the first stanza the speaker describes the cherry as "wearing white for Eastertide." Since white is the liturgical color for Easter, the tree is seen as celebrating the rebirth of Christ as well as the rebirth of the year. But the biblical association of the Easter metaphor leads the persona to the realization of his allotted "threescore years and ten," and his vision of a springtime world of rebirth is altered by his sudden sense of his own transience, so that in the last stanza he can only see the cherry as "hung with snow," reflecting the shift in point of view from a world of spring and rebirth to one of winter and death. "Hung" may also recall the Easter metaphor, though now it alludes not to resurrection but to death. Since the poem achieves its effect by its understatement, the burden of meaning must be carried by the structural pattern developed through the imagery.

The progressive pattern of imagery is one means of communicating a shift in perspective without the necessity of having the persona articulate his own understanding of the

process of change he is undergoing, and it is made necessary
by the essentially inarticulate nature of Housman's persona.
The device is used successfully in "Bredon Hill," where the
bells heard by the young lovers as wedding bells in
springtime become funeral bells in winter, a structural pattern which parallels the color imagery of "Loveliest of
Trees." The structure of "Bredon Hill" is more complex,
however, since the speaker continues the wedding image in
describing his love's death:

> But when the snows at Christmas
> On Bredon top were strown,
> My love rose up so early
> And stole out unbeknown
> And went to church alone.
>
> They tolled the one bell only,
> Groom there was none to see,
> The mourners followed after,
> And so to church went she,
> And would not wait for me.
> [ll. 21–30]

As does "Loveliest of Trees," the poem conveys a sense of
the persona's discovery of human transience which he is
himself incapable of describing. He views the girl's death as
if it were an act of conscious will, as if he has been betrayed
by his lover, who "stole out unbeknown," to meet another
suitor.[4] The conception of human transience which this
poem conveys thus comes not so much through the persona's understanding as through the reader's interpretation of
the speaker's more limited point of view. The persona's own
sense of loss and his awareness, at the end of the poem, that
the innocence and permanence of young love were illusory,
are voiced in an almost childish manner:

> The bells they sound on Bredon,
> And still the steeples hum.
> 'Come all to church, good people,'—
> Oh, noisy bells, be dumb;
> I hear you, I will come.
> [ll. 31–35]

The last line indicates that he is now aware that he too must

follow his love to church. The bells now toll only
death, but his perception is conveyed in a tone o
petulance: "Oh, noisy bells, be dumb." These are
described in the first stanza as "A happy noise to h
it is through the shifts in the poem's imagery and
ulations in tone as the poem develops that the final two lines
achieve their power.

It is, indeed, through the structural devices of his poetry
that Housman is enabled so frequently to invest the commonplace observations of his persona with some significance. The speaker's reaction to the sorrows of love in
"When I was one-and-twenty" culminates in the most unre-
markable line, "And oh, 'tis true, 'tis true," but the poem as a
whole succeeds in conveying a much more complex view of
the young man's insight into the nature of human affections.
Structurally, the poem plays off its two stanzas against one
another. The imagery of giving and spending dominates
both stanzas, but the full meaning of the imagery of the first
becomes clear only in its repetition in stanza 2. The advice of
the "wise man" on love to give "crowns and pounds and
guineas" goes unheeded by the lad of one-and-twenty, but
then its significance is not apparent, even to the reader:

> When I was one-and-twenty
>     I heard a wise man say,
> 'Give crowns and pounds and guineas
>     But not your heart away;
> Give pearls away and rubies
>     But keep your fancy free.'
> But I was one-and-twenty,
>     No use to talk to me.
>
>                         [ll. 1–8]

The theme of the poem—the notion that only experience
itself can correct the illusions held by the innocent youth—is
reflected perfectly in its structure. The meaning of the imagery of stanza 1 is hazy because it is reported from the point of
view of the naive listener of one-and-twenty. Why is love
discussed in monetary terms? Why must the fancy be kept
free? The metaphorical language and word play ("fancy
free") are puzzling until their repetition in the second
stanza, where the full implication of the imagery is made

clear only after the persona has passed from his innocent
state:

> When I was one-and-twenty
>     I heard him say again,
> 'The heart out of the bosom
>     Was never given in vain;
> 'Tis paid with sighs a plenty
>     And sold for endless rue.'
> And I am two-and-twenty,
>     And oh, 'tis true, 'tis true.
>
> [ll. 9–16]

Here is the same metaphor and even the word play (the pun
on *vein* in line 12), but the meaning is now clear. The heart
differs from pearls and crowns precisely because it cannot be
given away. It is always sold because the giver receives
something in return, and what he receives consists of the
sorrows which love inevitably entails. The fancy can be free
only by being kept. The cryptic words of the wise man were
not the puzzle they seemed, but their solution depended on
the persona's own experience. Structurally, the poem is
quite sophisticated in spite of its ingenuous persona; the
meaning unfolds only as the lad's knowledge advances, with
the final note of recognition occurring in the last line: "And
oh, 'tis true, 'tis true." In context, the line works very well,
since it provides the emotional counterpart to the words of
the wise man, which make their appeal only to the intellect.
The emotional outcry in the last line, because it is a product
of experience and thus "true," outweighs the rest of the
poem in its force, although it achieves its effect only because
the contrasts between one-and-twenty and two-and-twenty,
intellect and feeling, innocence and experience have been
set up in the preceding lines.

One sometimes has the impression that the poems of the
type discussed here exist only for that moment when the
persona utters the equivalent of "Oh, 'tis true," whether it is
the resolve to watch the cherry hung with snow or the words
spoken to the funeral bells, "I hear you, I will come." In "On
Wenlock Edge" that moment is contained in the line "Then
'twas the Roman, now 'tis I," which serves to bring the separate strands of the poem together. The structure of "On Wen-

lock Edge" has been examined in some detail by Spiro Peterson,[5] who notes that the poem is built on two dominant motifs. The first is the historical perspective of man as represented by the comparison of the English yeoman who now watches the storm on Wenlock Edge and the Roman he imagines as having observed the same scene when the hill was the site of the Roman city Uricon. The second motif, which parallels the first, is suggested primarily by the poem's imagery, and it involves the further correlation between man and nature. Both patterns are set out in the opening stanzas:

> On Wenlock Edge the wood's in trouble;
>   His forest fleece the Wrekin heaves;
> The gale, it plies the saplings double,
>   And thick on Severn snow the leaves.
>
> 'Twould blow like this through holt and hanger
>   When Uricon the city stood:
> 'Tis the old wind in the old anger,
>   But then it threshed another wood.
>
> Then, 'twas before my time, the Roman
>   At yonder heaving hill would stare:
> The blood that warms an English yeoman,
>   The thoughts that hurt him, they were there.
>                                     [ll. 1–12]

The yeoman's description of the natural setting, with the woods "in trouble" because of the wind's "old anger," carries the implication that nature reflects the plight of man. This correlation is strengthened in stanza 4 with the metaphors of "gale of life" and "tree of man." It is more than the conventional pathetic fallacy of nature poetry, for the speaker sees that, literally, man and nature are subject to the same life force. This force, which is represented by the wind, also serves to universalize the theme by linking Englishman and Roman, present and past. The first movement of the poem is thus a kind of expansion in which the private feelings of the persona are extended beyond himself in two directions—toward nature and back into the past. The movement serves as an escape from the privacy of the "thoughts that hurt him," but it is followed in stanza 4 by a contraction which brings the focus back to the speaker, though now with a new perspective:

> There, like the wind through woods in riot,
>    Through him the gale of life blew high;
> The tree of man was never quiet:
>    Then 'twas the Roman, now 'tis I.
>
> [ll. 13–16]

The studied understatement of the last line does not completely hide the persona's realization of the complex relationship of past and present, the generic plight of man and his own personal plight. The line suggests two conflicting moods, for it says both that his is a condition that all men must undergo and, conversely, that it is only in time, in the existing present, that the thoughts and feelings which trouble him have any significance. As in so many other Housman poems, the immediacy of feeling prevails finally, but the strategy of the poem's structure provides the necessary context in which the feelings are given meaning. It is curious that the poem ultimately implies the opposite of what it seems to be saying. It deals superficially with the universal subjugation of man and nature to a common fate, but its focus is on individual man, whose sense of that fate is what really matters to Housman. The final stanza extends the perspective of man and nature to the future in an indirect manner:

> The gale, it plies the saplings double,
>    It blows so hard, 'twill soon be gone:
> To-day the Roman and his trouble
>    Are ashes under Uricon.
>
> [ll. 17–20]

The storm will blow itself out, and to complete the parallel, the last two lines should be addressed to the speaker's future—soon he will be ashes under Uricon.[6] That is the sense of the poem's ending, but Housman again avoids a possibly maudlin conclusion by having the speaker project his own fate in terms of the impersonal past. It is an ambiguous ending. Is it comforting or painful to think that "then 'twas the Roman, now 'tis I"? The two moods are so mixed as to be indistinguishable. The focus of the poem is not on the speaker's reaction to his fate so much as on his realization of it. The triumph of the poem consists in the control of mood and tone, which are maintained through the concentration on the parallels of past and present, man and nature. In only one line of the poem are the speaker's feelings turned inward, yet the sense of his emotional turmoil and his contradictory passive acceptance of his brief role in the long process of generation is carried through the motifs of the troubled wood and the imaginary Roman and his trouble, now "ashes under Uricon."

Edith Sitwell is one of a number of readers who have voiced an objection to the rigidity and bareness of the structure of Housman's verse. She finds that

in most of Housman's poems, the place in which the stanzas are put might easily be transferred, and it would make little or no difference to the poem,—to passion and to meaning—and this shows that the form is not the result of a living force. I am unable to understand why Housman's technique should have been so much admired by some people. It is not actually incompetent, but it rarely bears the slightest relation to the subject.[7]

I have, of course, been arguing exactly the opposite, and in the poems discussed thus far it seems clear that the order of the stanzas could not be transferred without destroying the poem and, further, that the structure of the poem bears the closest possible relation to the subject. Miss Sitwell mentions "The Recruit" as an instance of the incompetence of Housman's structural devices, but the poem, on the contrary, seems to me a clear example of the manner in which the poet allows the structure to bear the burden of the poem's meaning. It is true that the statement of the poem is composed of the commonplaces typical of Housman's rustic persona:

> Leave your home behind, lad,
>     And reach your friends your hand,
> And go, and luck go with you
>     While Ludlow tower shall stand.
>
> Oh, come you home of Sunday
>     When Ludlow streets are still
> And Ludlow bells are calling
>     To farm and lane and mill,

> Or come you home of Monday
>    When Ludlow market hums
> And Ludlow chimes are playing
>    'The conquering hero comes',
>
> Come you home a hero,
>    Or come not home at all,
> The lads you leave will mind you
>    Till Ludlow tower shall fall.
>                        [ll. 1–16]

It is important to note, however, that the structure of the poem contrives to undermine the hopeful words of the persona to the young recruit. This is accomplished by the progressive repetition of the last line of stanza 1, which carries with it the suggestion of transience as it pictures the gradual decay of the tower which is being cited as a symbol of permanence.[8] It is not, I think, a totally successful poem, but whatever success it achieves depends on the irony generated by the development of the refrain as it works against the statement of the persona.

A more successful instance of a structural pattern which depends on the shifts in tone signalled by the repetition and modulation of a refrain line is in the opening poem of *A Shropshire Lad,* "1887." As is true of many of the early poems of *A Shropshire Lad,* the tone of the poem shifts from an early mood of celebration to a final recognition of some element which qualifies or destroys it. The note of celebration is reflected in the first two stanzas by the festive atmosphere surrounding the commemoration of Victoria's Golden Jubilee:

> From Clee to heaven the beacon burns,
>    The shires have seen it plain,
> From north and south the sign returns
>    And beacons burn again.
>
> Look left, look right, the hills are bright,
>    The dales are light between,
> Because 'tis fifty years to-night
>    That God has saved the Queen.
>                        [ll. 1–8]

Housman's use of variations on the phrase "God save the Queen" carries with it overtones of the traditional, unthinking attitude toward God and country assumed on such occasions. The development of the theme of "1887" depends, however, on the way in which the poem redefines the traditional phrase. In the second and third stanzas it is associated with the dead soldiers, "friends of ours / Who shared the work with God" (ll. 11–12). This association leads to an identification of the soldiers with Christ, since they perished to save others, and the persona speaks of them in terms which recall the mocking of Christ in New Testament accounts: "The saviours come not home to-night: / Themselves they could not save" (ll. 15–16). The term *save* has, of course, undergone an important transformation, being shifted from its theological sense to mean simply "preserve" or "maintain," and that is the direction in which the poem moves—from an innocent faith in the operation of some unseen benevolent power to a recognition that the generic permanence of man rests on the transience of individual man. The last two stanzas of the poem bring this progression to its final stage:

> 'God save the Queen' we living sing,
>     From height to height 'tis heard;
> And with the rest your voices ring,
>     Lads of the Fifty-third.
>
> Oh, God will save her, fear you not:
>     Be you the men you've been,
> Get you the sons your fathers got,
>     And God will save the Queen.
>                               [ll. 25–32]

The poem has been the subject of some critical controversy, which has centered on its tone. How are we to regard the apparently ironic treatment of a traditional, almost sacrosanct attitude? Housman denied that he was mocking the patriotism expressed in the poem,[9] and I am inclined to accept his statement at face value. The tone betrays no trace of sarcasm, and the function of Housman's redefinition of the phrase which expresses that patriotism is not mockery but the revelation of his persona's insight into the human condition in which patriotism finds its real meaning. The structure of the poem involves a process of revelation, and the repetition of the cant phrase in its different contexts carries the shifts in tone which reveal the growing insight of the persona. Shifting the burden of salvation from God to man does not lessen the speaker's admiration for the heroism involved in "saving" the queen, nor do I find the bitterness in his attitude which some commentators have noted. The final attitude is rather one of a recognition that the celebration of life is built on the foundation of death, a mood expressed so well in "Loveliest of Trees" when the persona resolves, after his sudden sense of mortality, to view the cherry, "hung with snow." The religious imagery of "1887" works in much the same manner as the nature imagery of "Loveliest of Trees." In both instances the structural development is dramatic, since its function is to capture the moment when the persona becomes aware of what is, for Housman, the most essential element of his consciousness. "1887" stands as the archetype of one of the most persistent structural patterns in Housman's poetry, though it is confined primarily to the first half of A Shropshire Lad.

The other pattern of development which influences most directly the shape of Housman's poetry begins to make its appearance in the second half of A Shropshire Lad, and it occurs frequently throughout the remainder of the collected poems. It depends heavily on the situation which Dylan Thomas exploits so well in lyrics like "Fern Hill"—the persona who remembers how it was to have been young and who captures in his memory of a blighted Eden the joy and pain of innocence as well as the gulf which now lies between him and his youth. In A Shropshire Lad this mood is signalled by the exile from the home shire and usually arises in the contrast between the Shropshire imagery, which recalls the state of innocence, and that implying the speaker's present exile:

> Into my heart an air that kills
> From yon far country blows:
> What are those blue remembered hills,
> What spires, what farms are those?

> That is the land of lost content,
>> I see it shining plain,
> The happy highways where I went
>> And cannot come again.
>>          [*A Shropshire Lad* XL][10]

The prevailing mood of *Last Poems* is that of the second half of *A Shropshire Lad,* where the persona muses on his Shropshire youth from a new vantage point and sees both the loss and gain involved in the process of change. "The First of May" (*Last Poems* XXXIV) exhibits one characteristic pattern of the exile poem. Its four stanzas are divided evenly between the two points of view it develops. In the first two stanzas the persona recaptures something of the sense of being a part of a world at its prime:

> The orchards half the way
>> From home to Ludlow fair
> Flowered on the first of May
>> In Mays when I was there;
> And seen from stile or turning
>> The plume of smoke would show
> Where fires were burning
>> That went out long ago.
>
> The plum broke forth in green,
>> The pear stood high and snowed,
> My friends and I between
>> Would take the Ludlow road;
> Dressed to the nines and drinking
>> And light in heart and limb,
> And each chap thinking
>> The fair was held for him.
>>          [ll. 1–16]

The imagery of the stanzas sustains the effect that the spring as well as the fair was being held for the young man. It reflects the sense of harmony with the flowering world which Housman achieves in his best nature poetry. Yet the sense of harmony is erased in the following stanzas, and we now see the distance between the persona and his lost youth. The distance is made real by the projection of other young men who are now "the fools that we were then":

Between the trees in flower
New friends at fairtime tread
The way where Ludlow tower
Stands planted on the dead.
Our thoughts, a long while after,
They think, our words they say;
Theirs now's the laughter,
The fair, the first of May.

Ay, yonder lads are yet
The fools that we were then;
For oh, the sons we get
Are still the sons of men.
The sumless tale of sorrow
Is all unrolled in vain:
May comes to-morrow
And Ludlow fair again.

[ll. 17–32]

The Wordsworthian harmony with nature developed in the first two stanzas has now become curiously depersonalized when seen from the point of view of the adult exiled from the natural world. It was all an illusion; neither the spring nor the fair existed for him, and he was a fool to think so. It was nothing more than a part in an endless pageant of foolish young men acting out their brief roles: "Our thoughts, a long while after, / They think, our words they say." But the new tough-mindedness cannot completely destroy the beauty of the former vision, and the persona betrays himself finally, for the illusion is stronger than the knowledge that it was an illusion: "The sumless tale of sorrow / Is all unrolled in vain." The poem returns in its last two lines to where it began: "May comes to-morrow / And Ludlow fair again." He may scoff at the fool he was then, but his heart lies with the young man who blithely takes the Ludlow road between the flowering orchards thinking the fair is held for him. Structurally, the poem reinforces the speaker's recognition of the "sumless" process of change, but it also conveys something of the manner in which the past is always present, though beyond reach—Tennyson's "Death in Life, the days that are no more." The poem would be no more than a diatribe against the follies of youth were it not successful in suggesting, through the contrast of its two points of view, the complexity of the relationship between past and present and the ambivalence of the persona's attitude toward the relationship.

Housman most successfully evokes a sense of the lost past through his nature imagery. In *Last Poems* XL, "Tell me not here, it needs not saying," nature, embodied in the changing seasons, is an enchantress who beguiled the young man into thinking she was his:

> Tell me not here, it needs not saying,
>   What tune the enchantress plays
> In aftermaths of soft September
>   Or under blanching mays,
> For she and I were long acquainted
>   And I knew all her ways.
>                       [ll. 1–6]

The tone is that of a love poem, and the lost sense of possessing nature is carried by sexual imagery. The point of view is that of the lover who looks back on a youthful affair from the vantage point of experience. He sees now that she was heartless and fickle, but he once possessed her. As in "The First of May," the mood is complicated by a blend of nostalgia for something beautiful which has been lost and the scornful attitude of maturity which belittles his earlier naiveté. The hint of sexuality pervades even the descriptions of seasonal change:

> On acres of the seeded grasses
>   The changing burnish heaves;
> Or marshalled under moons of harvest
>   Stand still all night the sheaves;
> Or beeches strip in storms for winter
>   And stain the wind with leaves.
>
> Possess, as I possessed a season,
>   The countries I resign,
> Where over elmy plains the highway
>   Would mount the hills and shine,
> And full of shade the pillared forest
>   Would murmur and be mine.
>                       [ll. 13–24]

In the final stanza the sexual imagery is made explicit. Nature is a harlot who wantonly bestows her favors on whatever stranger chances to encounter her. She is not merely heartless, she is witless; it is only the innocent, ignorant of the character of nature's mindlessness, who could believe he possessed her:

> For nature, heartless, witless nature,
>   Will neither care nor know
> What stranger's feet may find the meadow
>   And trespass there and go,
> Nor ask amid the dews of morning
>   If they are mine or no.
>
> [ll. 25–30]

Yet the young man did possess her, and the poem builds on the tension between the worlds of innocence and knowledge, both equally real. The later viewpoint does not cancel the former; it merely renders it more poignant. The disillusioned attitude of the world of knowledge controls the point of view, but the tone and imagery evoke the lost world of the adolescent. Although the speaker protests "it needs not saying," the tune the enchantress plays still beguiles him, and her music dominates the mood of the poem. It is a pattern—the simultaneous presentation of two conflicting moods—which Housman employs frequently in Last Poems.

The tone of "Tell me not here" also dominates the lyrics of Last Poems. The intrusion of the Edenic past into the fallen world is handled in a number of different ways, but almost always the persona is conscious of what it means to have been young and what it now means to have lost the vision of youth. It is as if Wordsworth should have recognized in his old age that the vision of nature he had celebrated in his best poems was illusory, a product of his youthful naiveté, although it is not quite that, since the disillusionment of Housman's persona is almost always conditioned by an element of praise. The poems are most successful, it seems to me, when the tension between past and present is felt but not resolved. It is the ambivalence of the state of adult exile which Housman best conveys in the lyrics of the second half of A Shropshire Lad and in Last Poems. When the bitterness or regret of the world of experience dominates the poem completely, the resulting tone seems thin, as in *Last Poems* XXVIII:

> Now dreary dawns the eastern light,
>     And fall of eve is drear,
> And cold the poor man lies at night,
>     And so goes out the year.
>
> Little is the luck I've had,
>     And oh, 'tis comfort small
> To think that many another lad
>     Has had no luck at all.

What is missing here is the tension found in the more successful lyrics of *Last Poems*. The tone of self-pity is too strong, but that is more a failure of technique than of sensibility. The poem is flat and thin not because the persona's feelings are unworthy of lyric poetry but because, structurally, the poem is inadequate to convey the depths of his feelings. The problem, essentially, is a reliance on statement rather than on form, and what the speaker tells us is neither supported by the poem's clichéd images of "dreary dawns" and "fall of eve" nor provided a context by the conflicting points of view found in such poems as "The First of May" and "Tell me not here." There is little of this sort of thing in *Last Poems*, much more, unfortunately, in *More Poems* and *Additional Poems*. And I must agree with Stephen Spender's judgment that the posthumous publication of these two collections does Housman a disservice, "because although they contain beautiful lines and even whole poems as good as any he wrote, they say in a cruder form, which sometimes amounts almost to parody, what he has said before."[11] It is, in fact, the crudeness of form which produces the effect of parody in many of the poems of the two posthumous collections. Although they repeat the dominant themes of *A Shropshire Lad* and *Last Poems*, they also illustrate the wisdom of Housman's dictum that poetry is not the thing said but a way of saying it.

The manner of expression explored most successfully in *Last Poems* depends a great deal on the point of view and structural patterns I have been describing. A number of the finest lyrics of *Last Poems* begin with the persona musing on his boyhood when he had "youth and pride." The point of view is colored by the irony almost always present in looking back on one's former self from the vantage point which time provides. The structural pattern involves the bringing together momentarily of two modes of seeing which have meaning primarily in relation to each other. *Last Poems* XXXIX provides an instance of this:

> When summer's end is nighing
>     And skies at evening cloud,
> I muse on change and fortune
>     And all the feats I vowed
>     When I was young and proud.
>
> The weathercock at sunset
>     Would lose the slanted ray,
> And I would climb the beacon
>     That looked to Wales away
>     And saw the last of day.
>
> From hill and cloud and heaven
>     The hues of evening died;
> Night welled through lane and hollow
>     And hushed the countryside,
>     But I had youth and pride.
>                                  [ll. 1–15]

The imagery of dying summer and dying day unites past and present, and structurally the poem is built on the two contrasting responses to an image that signals the death of something desirable. For the older man the image evokes the past, but ironically the vision that he conjures up is that of himself as a young man observing the same sunset and contemplating the future:

> The year might age, and cloudy
>     The lessening day might close,
> But air of other summers
>     Breathed from beyond the snows,
>     And I had hope of those.
>                                  [ll. 21–25]

Typically, Housman locates the essential difference between naiveté and experience in the attitude toward "change and fortune." The images of change, summer's end and sunset, recur in each stanza of the poem, and as the poem progresses the aspirations of the young man are replaced by the mature man's reluctant acceptance of what the scene he has gazed upon since boyhood really means. Typically, also, that meaning is underplayed, and the poem ends not with an outcry against the injustice of it all but with a simple sigh, the heart's echo of the last sounds of summer:

> So here's an end of roaming
> On eves when autumn nighs:
> The ear too fondly listens
> For summer's parting sighs,
> And then the heart replies.
> [ll. 31–35]

Reading in *Last Poems*, one notes how often the occasion for the poem is the search for the "lost young man," and further how often the poem turns, structurally, on the speaker's sense of his present state in terms of what he remembers of his youth. No poet since Wordsworth, with the possible exception of Thomas, has been so obsessed with the theme of the child as father of the man:

> When first my way to fair I took
> Few pence in purse had I,
> And long I used to stand and look
> At things I could not buy.
>
> Now times are altered: if I care
> To buy a thing I can;
> The pence are here and here's the fair,
> But where's the lost young man?
> [*Last Poems* XXXV, ll. 1–8]

The poems of this type all contain, at bottom, the paradoxical notion that it was only the illusion that made life meaningful. The mature man, in looking into the past, sees that life held a hope and a significance for the young man which he no longer finds. The very act of looking into the past destroys the meaning by revealing the illusion. In "When first my way to fair I took," this idea is suggested in a rather complex way by the contrast between the young man with the few pence for whom the fair held meaning, and the mature man, who could now satisfy the desires of his youth, except that the act would now be meaningless. It was only the vanity and innocence which created the desires (and the meaning), and the young man is gone. The fair itself, vanity fair, implies a view of the world as a kind of empty, glittering facade which attracts the country boy but dissolves into a tawdry sideshow when he returns to it as an adult. The poem's intent is not, however, to reveal the vanity of youthful desires but to suggest the destructive effect of knowledge:

> —To think that two and two are four
> And neither five nor three
> The heart of man has long been sore
> And long 'tis like to be.
>
> [ll. 9–12]

Whatever significance the fair held has departed with the lost young man, and the persona's search for meaning takes him back to the past to a meaning which is destroyed by the very act of observing it. The tension between past and present is obviously real for Housman, and it contains the sort of paradox which attracted him.

"Hell Gate" (*Last Poems* XXXI), a poem unlike any other Housman ever wrote, serves almost as an allegory for one aspect of his treatment of the past. In contrast to the poet's customary lyrical mode, "Hell Gate" employs narrative and symbolic devices to treat the convergence of idyllic past and hellish present. As the narrator journeys on the road to hell in the company of his "dark conductor," he reflects on the path which led him there:

> Many things I thought of then,
> Battle, and the loves of men,
> Cities entered, oceans crossed,
> Knowledge gained and virtue lost,
> Cureless folly done and said,
> And the lovely way that led
> To the slimepit and the mire
> And the everlasting fire.
>
> [ll. 25—32]

The sentry, one of the damned who guards the gates of hell,

also reminds him of another time and place, and in the company of Death and Sin, "the sentry turned his head, / Looked, and knew me, and was Ned" (ll. 63–64). At the center of the poem is the consequence of this vision from the past for the two old friends. United in hell, they revolt, and Ned turns his musket on the master of hell:

> And the hollowness of hell
> Sounded as its master fell,
> And the mourning echo rolled
> Ruin through his kingdom old.
> Tyranny and terror flown
> Left a pair of friends alone,
> And beneath the nether sky
> All that stirred was he and I.
> [ll. 87–94]

Then, silently, "nothing found to say," the two friends from the past begin "the backward way," and the hell-fire which has covered Ned begins to fade:

> And the ebbing lustre died
> From the soldier at my side,
> As in all his spruce attire
> Failed the everlasting fire.
> Midmost of the homeward track
> Once we listened and looked back;
> But the city, dusk and mute,
> Slept, and there was no pursuit.
> [ll. 97–104]

Clearly the poem deals with a recurring theme of *A Shropshire Lad* and *Last Poems*, a longing for the redemption of the fallen world by the innocent world of the past. It is a theme which could not be treated realistically, but the surrealistic atmosphere of "Hell Gate" allows the poet to realize a vision which is always destroyed in the surrounding lyrics of *Last Poems*—the return to the pastoral world of the early Shropshire poems. Ned, the symbol of that world, releases the persona from the hold of Death and Sin, the hell to which the fall from innocence has led him. At the end of the poem the two friends are on a "homeward track." The narrator has recovered the "lost young man," but only in a dream-vision.

A more typical treatment of the theme is that seen in the final lyric of *Last Poems*, "Fancy's Knell." The poem begins with the now-familiar recollection of the childhood world, then advances, as the shade advances over England in the poem's controlling image, to the darkened vision of the adult world:

> When lads were home from labour
> At Abdon under Clee,
> A man would call his neighbour
> And both would send for me.
> And where the light in lances
> Across the mead was laid,
> There to the dances
> I fetched my flute and played.
> [ll. 1–8]

As in the concluding two poems of *A Shropshire Lad*, the persona has assumed the role of the artist, although here he is not the poet but the pastoral musician. The shift is crucial in dictating the mood of the poet's farewell to his audience. At the end of Housman's first volume Terence had argued, in effect, that his verse was important since it outlasted time and prepared new generations of young men for all the troubles that the transient flesh is heir to. "Fancy's Knell," on the other hand, pursues the theme that the artists's tune has meaning only for the moment. The shift in imagery from poetry to music carries with it the suggestion that the music is lost in air the moment it is played, just as the musician is ultimately lost to the earth.

In addition to the customary contrast of past and present, the poem is built on the antithesis of air and earth, the unsubstantial joy of the moment and the inexorable movement of time. Both motifs are present from the beginning, contained in the initial setting in which the persona provides with his flute what are now seen as "idle pleasures" while the darkness envelops the earth:

> Ours were idle pleasures,
> Yet oh, content we were,
> The young to wind the measures,
> The old to heed the air;

> And I to lift with playing
>    From tree and tower and steep
> The light delaying,
>    And flute the sun to sleep.
>                    [ll. 9–16]

Implicit in the image are Housman's habitual themes of the
youth's sense of his mastery of the world and the speaker's
recognition of the vanity of that notion. Stanza 2 gives us the
young man's feeling that his music had power over the advance of time, but the distance provided by the poem's re-
trospective point of view allows us to see that just the opposite was true. Time held him green and dying as he sang in
his chains. Housman does not convey the paradoxical nature
of the theme with the immediacy that Thomas achieves; his
imagery suggests instead the steady advance of the darkness
and the brevity of the tune which seeks to delay it:

> Wenlock Edge was umbered,
>    And bright was Abdon Burf,
> And warm between them slumbered
>    The smooth green miles of turf;
> Until from grass and clover
>    The upshot beam would fade,
> And England over
>    Advanced the lofty shade.
>
> The lofty shade advances,
>    I fetch my flute and play:
> Come, lads, and learn the dances
>    And praise the tune to-day.
> To-morrow, more's the pity,
>    Away we both must hie,
> To air the ditty,
>    And to earth I.
>                    [ll. 25–40]

The advancing shade obscures the distance between past
and present even as it connects them, and the ditty that the
artist now plays tells us only of its own transience. The last
two lines unite two strands of the poem's imagery with a
finality that signals the end of the artist's public performance.

The theme of "Fancy's Knell," with its emphasis on the inconsequential nature of the artist's song, may indicate that Housman judged his public performance as worthy only of a fleeting notice. It is interesting, at any rate, that he reverses the convention of the permanence of art with which he concluded *A Shropshire Lad*. But his verse has achieved a permanent place in British poetry in spite of its modest claims. Clearly, his achievement is not based on the limited themes he chose to pursue—these are the commonplaces of much second- and third-rate verse—nor on his infamous view of life, which has worked against his reputation as a poet. It is based on his mastery of the craft of poetry, on the art by which he makes accessible an admittedly limited view of human life. He is almost entirely concerned with a view of the world confined to the young (or the old reflecting on youth), and he reveals it both from the point of view of the adolescent and that of the adult whose world has been permanently altered by the childhood vision. The strategies of Housman's poems are designed to allow us to share, at least momentarily, the sense of what it means to recognize the passing of youth, the movement from one view of life to another. It is, of course, a traditional rather than a modernist concern, and Housman's treatment of it struck his early readers as distinctly old-fashioned. It was, in fact, the nature of Housman's own art which helped condition the initial response of the thirties critics to *The Name and Nature of Poetry* and led consequently to the opinion still voiced of Housman as the heir of nineteenth-century poetic theory doing battle against the modernist movement represented by poets such as Eliot and Pound.

## Notes

1. Tom Burns Haber, *The Making of A Shropshire Lad* (Seattle: University of Washington Press, 1966), p. 22.
2. The reader may satisfy himself on this point by consulting Haber's *The Making of A Shropshire Lad*, which prints the existing drafts of the *Shropshire Lad* poems. I find it especially curious that

Haber should have given the impression that Housman was not a sensitive and demanding artist when he himself has reported so much evidence to the contrary; and I quote here at length several examples of Haber's descriptions of the drafts of well-known poems to counter the myth of Housman as the spontaneous artist whose poems appeared ready-made in his head. (A and B refer to two of four poetic notebooks left by Housman, now in the Library of Congress.)

Of the two drafts of "Is my team ploughing" Haber states: "The much-corrected writing on the remains of B 32 indicates that Housman's first essay at the poem was fraught with difficulty; however, the work of another day, although two or three months removed, must have recaptured all the impetus of the first moments of inspiration. The two stanzas that had proved unmanageable in the first draft—numbers 5 and 6—were the only ones that called for extensive rewriting; these and the six other quatrains of the poem were brought to the status of printer's copy on B 68 and 69. The painstaking care manifested in these entries testifies to Housman's absorption in this poem, which years later he thought might be his best" (p. 144).

Haber's description of the drafts of "To an Athlete Dying Young" reveals what the reprinted versions make clear—the final shape of the poem is almost entirely a product of rewriting: "Nowhere in the four notebooks does one obtain a better view of Housman's workshop method than in the two drafts of this poem. One can see his racing pen in motion over A 240 jotting down stanzas, couplets, single lines, seizing the separate fragments as they took shape in language. There we may now read, in this order, substantial forms of stanzas 1, 6, 3, and 7; the closing couplet of stanza 5, and the opening couplet of stanza 4. Here much was done, but much remained to do, for only seven lines on A 240 were carried intact into the second draft; however the theme of the poem was firmly established in the first and final quatrains." He concludes, "It is likely that the poem advanced measurably toward completeness on the next (now missing) page, for the entry on B 10–11 has the look of a page rewrought with the measured confidence of one who had sat down to deal with an approximately full-scale draft. Each quatrain is now complete and in its proper position although nearly every one shows traces of cancellation and rewriting. Below the last line of his final stanza, Housman immediately turned to two stanzas left unresolved on the preceding page and rewrote the fourth and the opening couplet of the fifth. Neither revision was altogether satisfactory, and a number of cruxes here and in other stanzas were left for later reckoning when printer's copy was in the making, eight months later" (p. 107).

Finally, in his description of the revision of "Twice a week the winter thorough" Haber demonstrates the art that transformed an unsatisfactory "inspiration" into a unified poem: "It is apparent in the draft that the labor of revision in this three-stanza poem centered upon the opening stanza. After making numerous interlineations and rewriting line 2 in the right margin twice, Housman, still dissatisfied, continued on the following page, B 27, his efforts to bring about the refractory line. Before he closed his notebook he had before him among the alternatives the line that was to go into print, although it is doubtful that he recognized it this early in the none-too-assured writing and the maze of cancel-strokes." Haber then goes on to describe other crucial substitutions which "produce a sense of unity that was lacking in the original version" (p. 99).

These are not, I should add, untypical examples. A study of the manuscript revisions reprinted in *The Making of A Shropshire Lad* tells us more about Housman's craft than could hundreds of pages of critical commentary. Unfortunately, although he has provided the evidence of the art Housman exercised in composing his verse, Haber was not able to do much with it. Nevertheless, the book is of great value as a record of Housman's careful craftsmanship.

3. See *Housman's Land of Lost Content: A Critical Study of A Shropshire Lad* (Knoxville: University of Tennessee Press, 1970).

4. As Cleanth Brooks notes in "Alfred Edward Housman," pp. 72–73. I am indebted to Brooks's reading of the poem.

5. "Housman's 'On Wenlock Edge,' " *Explicator* 15 (1956–57), Item 46.

6. As Peterson notes, the "sense of the complete parallel, the logic of the poem, the structure of the stanza demand the poem conclude with the same three words. . . . All the more conspicuous for their absence are the expected words, 'now 'tis I.' "

7. Osbert, Edith, and Sacheverell Sitwell, "Three Eras of Modern Poetry" in *Trio* (London: Macmillan, 1938), p. 105.

8. I have examined this poem and several others mentioned here at greater length in *Housman's Land of Lost Content*, and I repeat some of the points made earlier because these poems provide such clear examples of the structural principles under discussion.

9. See Brooks, "Alfred Edward Housman," p. 76.

10. See Chapter 7, "The Exile Poems," in *Housman's Land of Lost Content*, pp. 108–130.

11. See Spender's review, quoted in Richards, *Housman 1897–1936*, p. 369.

# 6
# HOUSMAN AND ELIOT: *A Note on Critical Fashion in the Thirties*

By THE TIME of the publication of *The Name and Nature of Poetry*, Housman's place in modern poetry had been fixed by the most influential groups of writers and critics of the thirties. For the poets of Pound's critical persuasion, for the Auden group, and for the *Scrutiny* critics, Housman was one of the last respectable survivors of a defunct poetic tradition, largely untouched by contemporary developments. Ezra Pound sounded the keynote in 1934 when he observed that there was no indication that Housman was even aware of the new literary world created by contemporary poets and critics.[1] In 1935, C. Day Lewis pictured Housman as one of his own pastoral figures, "flinging round him a mantle of stoicism" and breaking "into a pure, unrivalled burst of song, the last lyric ecstasy we were to hear for many a long day."[2] Day Lewis saw Housman as the "naif poet," the writer who "may have a close acquaintance with other poets, dead and living, yet remain as a poet almost untouched by them."[3] To Louis MacNeice he was an "escapist," the "English Romantic masochistically practising heroics in the last ditch."[4] And although Day Lewis, MacNeice, even Auden, expressed a qualified approval of Housman's "pure" lyrics, Auden going so far as to imitate some of Housman's rhetorical turns,[5] they were never able to take him quite seriously as a contemporary. Auden's sonnet "A. E. Housman," published in 1939, depicted him as a literary curiosity:

Deliberately he chose the dry-as-dust,
Kept tears like dirty postcards in a drawer;
Food was his public love, his private lust
Something to do with violence and the poor.
                                    [ll. 5–8][6]

The appearance of *Last Poems* in the year of *The Waste Land* had revealed, to these critics at least, the distance between Housman's pastoral English countryside and Eliot's "Unreal city."

The publication of *The Name and Nature of Poetry* thus served to reemphasize two poetic traditions of the thirties represented in the popular mind by Housman and Eliot. Since the lecture was seen on both sides as a veiled attack on the newer fashions of poetry and criticism, the notice it attracted was greater than that warranted by any disinterested attention to Housman's theory of poetry. In June 1933, the *London Mercury* applauded the lecture as "a bugle-call or the All Clear signal after an air-raid." Using Housman's remarks as the occasion for an attack on contemporary poetic practice, the reviewer stated that "during at least ten years, the field of poetry and poetical criticism has been invaded by swarms of people who haven't the least conception as to what poetry is, and who have affixed the name to things which have no relation at all to what has been called poetry through all the long past."[7] In February 1934, James Agate, the literary critic of the *Daily Express*, prophesied that Eliot might "Pound away" but that Housman would outlive them both.[8] The *Times* reviewer had been more circumspect, but his notice the day after the lecture had also sounded a note of triumph: "When the whole lecture is published . . . and this very dogmatic, academic age . . . learns the full sacrilege of Mr. Housman's remarks upon Donne and the metaphysicals, upon Dryden, and upon Pope, there will be some pretty outcries—or perhaps a dignified and discreet silence."[9]

The *Scrutiny* critics, whose leader F. R. Leavis had been singled out as one of the targets of Housman's attack, were not slow in responding. The September 1933 number contained two notices of the lecture and of the journalistic interest it had generated. Gorley Putt, reviewing the published version, dismissed it in a paragraph but lingered over the issue it had raised: "Far more noteworthy than the lecture itself as a sign of the times has been the concerted yelping of the higher-journalist critics to which it gave excuse. It would have been over-sanguine to expect much lively criticism of English poetry from a professor of Latin, but Mr. Housman's qualifications were such that his most jocular utterances have been echoed with solemnity."[10] Yet the issue, as he saw it, was simply that of old-fashioned as opposed to modern tastes in poetry: "Cultured people who feel that *The Shropshire Lad* [sic] is . . . the last appearance of the real thing in modern poetry have welcomed this pamphlet as making it safe for them to be quite explicit about the state of their taste. There has been a good deal of amusing explicitness."[11]

In their editorial comment in the same number, D. W. Harding and L. C. Knights saw a similar but somewhat more important issue implicit in Housman's lecture and the response it had prompted:

There is, of course, room for a good deal of difference of opinion about the merits of contemporary writers and their relative importance for the future. All the same, one could hardly be anything but amused by the trumpeting with which the *London Mercury*, in its June editorial, turned out the Old Guard against the Reactionaries—those who have reacted, that is, against the traditions of late nineteenth century poetry. Professor Housman's lecture on *The Name and Nature of Poetry* provided the occasion.[12]

Significantly, Harding and Knights go on to relate the lecture and its reception to a more fundamental sign of the times—a concentrated attack on the poetry and criticism of T. S. Eliot. The remainder of their comment catalogs similar attacks from the daily press, public lectures, and journals, and it concludes with a defense of Eliot and a plea for "sensitive and exact literary criticism": "The recent outbreak of derogatory articles will not provide that. They for the most part reveal nothing beyond their authors' thankfulness at being able safely now to set aside the writer whose work implicitly condemns their own shoddiness of thought and feeling."[13]

The battle lines had thus been drawn between the Old Guard and the Reactionaries, and, implicitly, between the two most prominent (at the moment) representatives of these two camps, Housman and Eliot. In regard to the nature of their poetry, there was certainly some justice in the division, but in terms of their critical theories the issue was not nearly so clear-cut. The controversy surrounding the Leslie Stephen Lecture had, in fact, created the misleading impression—still current—that Housman's and Eliot's conceptions of poetry represented two opposing schools. Both Housman's defenders and his detractors had been prepared to interpret *The Name and Nature of Poetry* (as they had used Housman's verse) to reinforce such an opposition. Yet, in doing so, they had ignored or misread the critical views of Eliot himself. Eliot's own response to the Leslie Stephen Lecture was set down in a review published in *The Criterion* in October 1933. The following month marked the publication of Eliot's Charles Eliot Norton Lectures, delivered at Harvard in 1932–33. These also contain several references to Housman's theory and his account of the composition of his poetry, Eliot having read Housman's work in the interval between the delivery and publication of the Norton Lectures. The Norton Lectures, however, are more important as an indication of the state of Eliot's own conception of poetry and criticism in 1933, and a careful reader of the two poets' views would have been hard-pressed to place them in opposing camps.

Shortly after Eliot's review of *The Name and Nature of Poetry* appeared, Housman sent a copy to his sister Katherine Symons with the comment that it was "amusing, because its author, T. S. Eliot, is worshipped as a god by the writers in the paper which had the only hostile review."[14] Housman was obviously struck by the irony of the situation; Eliot, who was being defended by the *Scrutiny* critics as the leader of the opposition, had applauded Housman and his performance rather extravagantly. The review opens with high praise indeed. Eliot nominates Housman as "one of the few living masters of English prose," and he states further that "on those subjects on which he chooses to exercise his talents, there is no one living who can write better."[15] The first third of the review is, in fact, devoted to an analysis of Housman's prose style, which is characterized in Eliot's view by "the intensity of the artist":

Mr. Housman's prose owes its distinction to the power which separates all first-class prose from the merely efficient: a certain emotional intensity. I say 'a certain' merely as a reminder that you cannot abstract completely an identity recognizable in all great prose. Nor is this intensity to be confounded with explicit emotion arising from or suitably infused into the subject-matter, such as indignation, scorn or enthusiasm. It is the intensity of the artist, and is capable of informing any subject-matter, even the most abstract, the most arid, or the most impersonal, narrative, expository, or scientifically descriptive. The present subject, however, gives Mr. Housman a wider range than those with which he is accustomed to deal; for he is both a nineteenth (or twentieth) century romantic poet and an eighteenth-century wit; and here, in his appreciation and his expression, he is able to expose both aspects in happy union.[16]

Those accustomed to reading between the lines would have noted that Eliot praises Housman as a prose writer rather than as a poet (Housman had characterized the literature of the eighteenth century in much the same fashion) and that he shows some hesitancy in admitting Housman into the twentieth century. Yet Eliot was, after all, reviewing a work of prose, and Housman had based his own reputation on his scholarly prose. The second distinction merely echoed the view of Eliot's circle that Housman's poetry belonged to the tradition of nineteenth-century romanticism. Housman, one would suspect, accepted that designation as "technically correct" but "essentially inappropriate."[17]

When he comes to the substance of Housman's remarks on poetry, Eliot finds himself unable to agree totally or to disagree, though he tends on the whole to defend Housman's statements, given the occasion of their utterance:

We must keep in mind that this essay is a lecture; and the exigencies of a popular lecture require the author to select his points very carefully, to aim at form and proportion rather than connected profundity, and to avoid going too deeply into anything which is, for the purposes of the moment, another problem. We must not, in short, judge a lecture on Poetry as if it was a book of Aesthetics. The author may himself walk the straight line, but if he is to say anything at all in the time it is difficult for him, if not impossible, not to make assertions which, if pressed firmly and indefatigably by an unfriendly critic, will not yield a concentrated drop of heresy. I think that such a critic might be able to extract (1) the Essence of Poetry Theory, (2) the Pure Poetry Theory, (3) the Physiological Theory. None of these theories can be flatly denied without equal error; I do not believe that Mr. Housman maintains any of them to a vicious degree; I mention them in the hope of sparing other critics the trouble of denouncing Mr. Housman for what he does not maintain.[18]

There is, to be sure, a note of condescension here (that is, it is only a lecture, and Housman does not maintain his theories to a vicious degree), yet Eliot finds more areas of agreement than disagreement with Housman's statements. He feels "a certain sympathy with Mr. Housman's acid comments on the poetry of the seventeenth and eighteenth centuries" because he suspects that "both have lately been for some amateurs a fashion rather than a taste"; he is, however, "more than doubtful" about Housman's attempt to separate the poetry and the wit in the metaphysicals. Housman's quotations in the lecture "show about as sensitive and refined perception as any human being can aspire to," but he is not quite fair to Dryden and Blake. Eliot would not like to deny Housman's assertation that "meaning is of the intellect, poetry is not," but neither would he wish to affirm it. There is, in short, "probably no ground for taking issue with Mr. Housman," yet Eliot cannot dismiss the subject "without at least affirming the extraordinary complexity of the problem, and the mazes of intellectual subtlety into which it is bound to lead the conscientious enquirer."[19] This last assertion justly characterizes Eliot's response to the conception of poetry articulated by Housman: it cannot be contradicted, but the issues are more complex than Housman was able to show in the scope of the lecture.

There is, however, one point on which Eliot is able to offer unqualified assent. The description of the composition of his poetry with which Housman concluded the lecture obviously struck a responsive chord in Eliot, and he offers it as evidence of the authenticity of Housman's poetry:

Mr. Housman has given us an account of his own experience in writing poetry which is important evidence. Observation leads me to believe that different poets may compose in different ways; my experience (for what that is worth) leads me to believe that Mr.

Housman is recounting the authentic processes of a real poet. 'I have seldom,' he says, 'written poetry unless I was rather out of health.' I believe that I understand that sentence. If I do, it is a guarantee—if any guarantee of that nature is wanted—of the quality of Mr. Housman's poetry.[20]

Eliot's rather odd conclusion suggests that his own experience in writing poetry parallels that given by Housman (and a passage in the Norton Lectures confirms this), yet in basing the authenticity of Housman's poetry on the physical state of the poet at the moment of creation Eliot seems to be echoing the physiological theory he had earlier detected with some misgivings in Housman. But this is only one of a number of issues which are clarified by an examination of Eliot's Norton Lectures. The review shows Eliot's admiration for the quality of Housman's prose (not unlike his own) as well as a more qualified endorsement of his poetry. The Norton Lectures provide the basis for a comparison of the two poets' critical views offered at approximately the same time.

I should make it clear, however, that in pursuing the parallels between Housman's and Eliot's conceptions of poetry and criticism in the thirties I am not attempting to strengthen the validity of Housman's theories by comparing them to the more influential pronouncements of Eliot. Neither am I endeavoring to add luster to Housman's reputation by placing him in the same theoretical camp as Eliot. I am rather attempting to correct the widely held view that Housman's statements on poetry and criticism do not deserve to be taken seriously, that they are hopelessly old-fashioned and have no place in our study of twentieth-century poetics. One method of correcting this view is to demonstrate that Housman's theories parallel in all essential details those of the man whose influence has dominated the taste of this century and, further, that Housman's ideas were dismissed in the thirties and subsequently not because of a careful scrutiny of the issues but because intellectual fashion dictated Eliot's role as founding father of modernism and relegated Housman to the position of nineteenth-century relic. It is significant that the close parallels between Housman's and Eliot's almost simultaneous pronouncements have never been examined in any detail, although in the published version of the Norton Lectures Eliot himself recognized crucial similarities and took pains to point them out.

Published as *The Use of Poetry and the Use of Criticism,* the eight Charles Eliot Norton Lectures were delivered at Harvard during the winter of 1932–33. Eliot describes them rather cavalierly as "a few light sketches to indicate the changes in the self-consciousness of poets thinking about poetry."[21] More specifically, they examine "the varying conceptions of the use of poetry during the last three centuries, as illustrated in criticism, and especially in the criticism provided by the poets themselves" (UP, p. 32).[22] Eliot's subject is thus the relation of criticism to poetry, but not merely that, since he begins with the assumption that "we do not know what poetry is, or what it does or ought to do, or what use it is," and his attempt is "to find out, in examining the relation of poetry and criticism, what the use of both of them is" (UP, p. 15). In short, where Housman had attempted to discover the essence of poetry, its name and nature, Eliot tries to reach poetry through criticism. The more cautious of the two, he refuses to be tied to any one definition of poetry, and he carefully qualifies his statements on poetry and criticism. The lectures are also quite loose in structure, and Eliot wanders freely over a number of vaguely related topics. Consequently, it is more difficult than with Housman to define any consistent approach in Eliot's criticism; his statements are suggestive rather than definitive, for, as he says in the concluding lecture, "I have no general theory of my own" (UP, p. 143).

Given the broad subjects of the two lecturers, it is not merely by chance that they cover much the same ground. Reviewing the two published works together in 1934, James Southall Wilson noted some superficial similarities, finding Eliot "nearer Housman than Arnold in what he demands of poetry" and seeing "interesting agreements" in the two poets' conceptions of meaning in poetry.[23] Eliot also noted the similarities, for in preparing his lectures for publication he added four references to Housman's *Name and Nature of Poetry,* which he had apparently read soon after his return from Harvard in June 1933. There are indeed a number of superficial parallels. Both poets quote Coleridge's statement that "poetry gives most pleasure when only generally and not perfectly understood"; both refer to Arnold's statement on the "Wordsworthians" who praise their poet for the wrong reasons; both offer explanations (though quite different ones) for the coarsening of poetic sensibilities in the eighteenth century. They agree, moreover, on the small number of readers capable of appreciating poetry to any real extent and make the same distinction, in identical terms, between "sham" poetry and the genuine article. More substantive parallels may, however, be seen in three issues central to both works—conceptions of criticism and of the critic, the question of meaning in poetry, and the nature of poetic "inspiration" or creativity.

Although he does not mention any modern critic by name, Housman's lecture was interpreted from the first as an attack on certain conceptions of criticism, particularly those of I. A. Richards and the young Cambridge critics and F. R. Leavis and the *Scrutiny* school. This impression was furthered by reports that the lecture had upset many of the Cambridge critics,[24] as well as the remark attributed to Richards: "This has put us back ten years."[25] Housman's conception of poetry as impervious to the intellect was unacceptable to critics like Richards who were associated with the newer sciences of psychology and sociology and to those who were attempting to define harder and more objective criteria for poetic analysis and evaluation. In denying the efficacy of intellectual and scientific criticism, Housman was reduced to the traditional conception of the literary critic as a man of taste. The intellect, he says, "is not the fount of poetry"; "it may actually hinder its production . . . and it cannot even be trusted to recognise poetry when produced" (SP, p. 188). The emphasis is instead on "the sensibility or insensibility of the percipient" (SP, p. 184). The literary critic may test his qualifications for the task set before him by asking such questions as these: "Am I capable of recognising poetry if I come across it? Do I possess the organ by which poetry is perceived?" (SP, p. 184). The organ of poetic appreciation is not specified, although Housman alludes to a number of physical sensations in his own experience as a reader, including a bristling of the skin, a shiver down the spine, a constriction of the throat, a precipitation of water to the eyes, and a sensation in the pit of the stomach. Whatever the organ by which poetry is perceived, it is obviously not the brain.

Such a nonintellectual conception of criticism was also seen as an attack on the criticism of Eliot. The *London Mercury* review of Housman's lecture had referred to "Dons . . . who have tried to analyse the unanalysable, . . . alleged poets and critics who test poems by their intellectual content," and Harding and Knights, responding in *Scrutiny*, interpreted the review as "showing a recrudescence of animus against Mr. Eliot."[26] If their interpretation was indeed correct, it merely points up the misunderstanding on both sides of Eliot's own view of criticism, for the Norton Lectures reveal a notion of the limits of criticism as circumscribed as that of Housman. In the opening lecture, Eliot defines criticism as "that department of thought which either seeks to find out what poetry is, what its use is, what desire it satisfies, why it is written, and why read, or recited; or which, making some conscious or unconscious assumptions that we do know these things, assesses actual poetry" (*UP*, p. 16). Yet this high purpose is never actually achieved, for criticism "never does find out what poetry is. . . . Nor can criticism ever arrive at any final appraisal of poetry" (*UP*, p. 16). Theoretically, then, criticism attempts to answer two questions—"what is poetry?" and "is this a good poem?" But the first question is unanswerable, and "no theoretic ingenuity will suffice to answer the second question, because no theory can amount to much which is not founded upon a direct experience of good poetry" (*UP*, p. 16).

For Eliot, as for Housman, the critic is ultimately reduced to his own taste, acquired from a lifetime of exposure to "the best literature of several languages," in Housman's phrase. "In order to analyse the enjoyment and appreciation of a good poem," Eliot states, "the critic must have experienced the enjoyment, and he must convince us of his taste" (*UP*, p. 17). Further, if "you had no faith in the critic's ability to tell a good poem from a bad one, you would put little reliance upon the validity of his theories" (*UP*, p. 17). Theory of whatever kind (Eliot alludes specifically to "scientific" criticism, psychological and sociological) must take second place to genuine taste, "founded on genuine feeling," and "inextricable from the development of the personality and character" (*UP*, p. 35).[27] It is true that personal taste is liable to error, "but we are all, as a matter of fact, imperfect people; and the man whose taste in poetry does not bear the stamp of his particular personality, so that there are differences in what he likes from what we like, as well as resemblances, and differences in the way of liking the same things, is apt to be a very uninteresting person with whom to discuss poetry" (*UP*, p. 36).

Such a reliance on taste is of course based on the assumption, made by both Housman and Eliot, that literary criticism is neither a science nor an inquiry subject to objective standards. This assumption is implicit in Housman's careful distinctions between science and criticism, the intellect and the emotions, and it leads to his somewhat exaggerated defense of subjectivism in literary criticism. Eliot's own view is stated more bluntly: "Alas, philosophy is not science, nor is literary criticism; and it is an elementary error to think that we have discovered as objective laws what we have merely imposed by private legislation" (*UP*, p. 60). It is in this connection that I. A. Richards plays such a prominent role in the lectures of both poets, in Housman by implication and by rumor after the fact, in Eliot more directly. Eliot's discussion of Richards's criticism makes explicit what Housman merely implies—the error of substituting for personal taste critical values based on a "scientific" system.

Eliot's treatment of Richards as a representative modern critic is not totally unsympathetic. Although he is unable to accept Richards's theory of value ("I cannot accept any such theory which is erected upon purely individual-psychological foundations" *UP*, p. 17), he obviously respects Richards's judgment and taste: "You may be dissatisfied with his philosophical conclusions but still believe (as I do) in his discriminating taste in poetry" (*UP*, p. 17). That Richards is, in Eliot's view, a good critic in spite of his scientific approach is, however, faint praise, since Eliot denies him the very foundation of his critical approach. He later implies that the importance of Richards's position in twentieth-century criticism may lie in his role in hastening the end of the very school which Richards represents:

> Whether we agree or not with any or all of his conclusions, whether we admit or deny that his method is adequate, we must admit that the work of Mr. I. A. Richards will have been of cardinal importance in the history of literary criticism. Even if his criticism proves to be entirely on the wrong track, even if this modern 'self-consciousness' turns out to be only a blind alley, Mr. Richards will have done something in accelerating the exhaustion of the possibilities. He will have helped indirectly to discredit the criticism of persons qualified neither by sensibility nor by knowledge of poetry, from which we suffer daily. There is some hope of greater clarity; we should begin to learn to distinguish the appreciation of poetry from theorising about poetry, and to know when we are not talking about poetry but about something else suggested by it. [UP, p. 123]

Eliot had earlier quoted Richards's statement on the "equipment the scientific critic needs": " 'both a passionate knowledge of poetry and a capacity for dispassionate psychological analysis' " (UP, p. 17). It is clear that he can accept only the first qualification and is attempting here to discredit the second.

Eliot's attack on Richards's criticism occupies a good part of his penultimate lecture, entitled "The Modern Mind." Richards, as a representative modern critical mind, exhibits both the modern tendency toward self-consciousness and the tendency to substitute scientific knowledge for traditional values. Of Richards's approach to poetry, Eliot says: "We may wonder whether it will lead the ordinary aspirant to understanding of good poetry. It is just as likely, I suspect, to confirm him in his taste for the second rate" (UP, p. 134). Finally, Eliot's distrust of Richards's criticism may be located not only in the specific theory which Richards advances, but also in the very fact that he relies on a theory of poetic value. In his concluding lecture Eliot admits to having no general theory of his own, and he warns us against the dangers of substituting theory for sensibility:

> It is reasonable, I feel, to be on guard against views which claim too much for poetry, as well as to protest against those which claim too little; to recognise a number of uses for poetry, without admitting that poetry must always and everywhere be subservient to any one

of them. And while theories of poetry may be tested by their power of refining our sensibility by increasing our understanding, we must not ask that they serve even that purpose of adding to our enjoyment of poetry; any more than we ask of ethical theory that it shall have a direct application to and influence upon human behaviour. [*UP*, p. 143]

We are back, then, to the assumption with which we began: the sine qua non of criticism is the personal, perhaps even eccentric, taste of the critic. "Even the most accomplished of critics," Eliot says, "can, in the end, only point to the poetry which seems to him to be the real thing" (*UP*, p. 18). Criticism is ultimately refined to the "sensibility or insensibility of the percipient" (*SP*, p. 184).

It is difficult to locate any essential difference between the concepts of criticism in Housman and Eliot, at least in 1933. Whatever the reasons for the outcry which greeted *The Name and Nature of Poetry* and which prompted the defense of Eliot from Housman's supposed attack, they cannot have been based on a thoughtful comparison of the two poets' views of the nature of criticism. This issue is, further, related to another aspect of Housman's theory that was also seen as an attack on the "intellectualist school" which included Eliot.[28] Housman had been interpreted as saying that meaning was inessential to poetry, and certainly a number of his statements suggest this interpretation. He doubts, for example, that there are "any such things as poetical ideas" (*SP*, p. 186); consequently, poetry "is not the thing said but a way of saying it" (*SP*, p. 187). "Meaning," he states, "is of the intellect, poetry is not," and "when poetry has a meaning, as it usually has, it may be inadvisable to draw it out" (*SP*, p. 187). Taken out of context, these remarks and others could be seen as an attempt to deny any significance to poetic meaning, yet that is not quite the case.

Shortly after the lecture, when Housman recognized that his statements on meaning had been misinterpreted, he wrote to his brother Laurence: "I did not say that poetry was the better for having no meaning, only that it can best be detected so."[29] This correction reminds us that the section of the lecture in which Housman's statements on meaning are found is concerned with describing the essential nature of

poetry. Here is the crucial passage: "Poetry is not the thing
said but a way of saying it. Can it then be isolated and
studied by itself? for the combination of language and its
intellectual content, its meaning, is as close a union as can
well be imagined. Is there such a thing as pure unmingled
poetry, poetry independent of meaning?" (SP, p. 187).
Housman never answers this question directly, but he does
imply that poetry may be enjoyed and appreciated independent of meaning, and he attempts to detect the essential poetic element (earlier characterized as a transfusion of emotion) by disregarding the meaning in several passages from
Shakespeare and Blake. It is Blake who most closely approximates "pure" poetry, and Housman says of him: "Blake,
again and again, as Shakespeare now and then, gives us
poetry neat, or adulterated with so little meaning that nothing except poetical emotion is perceived and matters" (SP, p.
189). Yet Housman recognizes that even those passages in
Blake which he cites as "pure and self-existent poetry" possess a meaning, although "the meaning is a poor foolish
disappointing thing in comparison with the verses themselves" (SP, p. 191).

Housman also acknowledges that Blake is a rather special
case, and he does not demand Blake's purity from all poetry:
"In most poets, as I said, poetry is less often found thus
disengaged from its usual concomitants, from certain things
with which it naturally unites itself and seems to blend in-
distinguishably" (SP, p. 192). Housman's remarks on meaning (and on Blake) were misunderstood partly because his
audience failed to distinguish between an attempt to detect
the essential poetic element and a value judgment concerning pure poetry. But Housman does not say that Blake is a
greater poet than Shakespeare, and he does not say, as he
reminds us, that poetry is better for having no meaning.
Blake is singled out only because he exhibits in a purer form
the poetic element Housman has been attempting to isolate.
Furthermore, Housman suggests in the passage quoted
above that in most cases the emotional element he defines as
essential to poetry cannot be separated from meaning, which
would indicate that there is rarely such a thing as poetry
independent of meaning. He also acknowledges the influ-

ence of the thought or meaning on the emotion transmitted by poetry. He comments on a passage from Wordsworth's *Prelude* by stating, "The feeling with which these lines are read is composite, for one constituent is supplied by the depth and penetrating truth of the thought" (SP, p. 192); and of Emerson's quatrain "Sacrifice" he says, "Much of the emotion kindled by that verse can be referred to the nobility of the sentiment" (SP, p. 192).[30] Housman thus is far from denying the significance of meaning in poetry; at the same time, his conception of poetry as a transfusion of emotion does not place a high premium on meaning as an indication of value. And this attitude is entirely consistent with his notion of criticism; just as the critic's intellectual equipment may get in the way of his natural sensibility, an undue emphasis on meaning may well extinguish the sensual pleasure of the poem.

Eliot's review of *The Name and Nature of Poetry* had singled out Housman's account of meaning and his discussion of Blake for special consideration, and his reaction suggests not so much a fundamental disagreement as an unwillingness to accept Housman's rather broad categories of meaning, physical, and intellectual. The key passage, to which I have already alluded, is this:

Mr. Housman's quotations, in this lecture, show about as sensitive and refined a perception as any human being can aspire to. But, in this way, is he quite fair to Dryden? and what is more important, for here he is concerned with a poet for whom he feels almost unqualified admiration, is he quite fair to Blake? I am sure that Blake would not be happy about it, but we have not here to do with Blake's feelings, but with the Problem of Meaning. There is probably no ground for taking issue with Mr. Housman; and I have no space here to develop the difficulties involved in any theory; but I cannot leave the subject without at least affirming the extraordinary complexity of the problem, and the mazes of intellectual subtlety into which it is bound to lead the conscientious enquirer. 'Meaning is of the intellect, poetry is not.' I should not like to deny this, still less to assert it; I am in the same quandary as Mr. Housman is with Pope. For what do we mean by meaning? and what by intellect? 'Poetry indeed seems to me more physical than intellectual.' Well, here again, is something I should not like to deny; but I am not sure I know what 'physical' and 'intellectual' mean.[31]

Eliot, of course, had written this shortly after giving his own account of poetic meaning in the Norton Lectures, and that account is surprisingly closer to Housman's position than the review would indicate. Eliot, it is true, is a much more cautious critic than Housman, and his discussion of meaning is hedged about with qualifications and restrictions. Reduced to its essentials, however, it is simply a more careful articulation of Housman's position.

Eliot is led to a consideration of the question of meaning in two different contexts in the Norton Lectures. The first involves the related problem of belief; the second, the problem of obscurity. In his consideration of Shelley and Keats in the fifth lecture, Eliot is moved to admit his own antipathy to Shelley's poetry, which involves directly the question of belief, indirectly the question of meaning. It is Shelley's ideas that Eliot finds abhorrent, and in searching for reasons for his dislike of Shelley's verse Eliot arrives at a conclusion which parallels Housman's view (quoting Coleridge) that "poetry gives most pleasure when only generally and not perfectly understood" since "perfect understanding will sometimes almost extinguish pleasure" (SP, p. 187). Eliot, who later quotes Coleridge's statement himself, writes:

I am inclined to think that the reason why I was intoxicated by Shelley's poetry at the age of fifteen, and now find it almost unreadable, is not so much that at that age I accepted his ideas, and have since come to reject them, as that at that age 'the question of belief or disbelief,' as Mr. Richards puts it, did not arise. It is not so much that thirty years ago I was able to read Shelley under an illusion which experience has dissipated, as that because the question of belief or disbelief did not arise I was in a much better position to enjoy the poetry. [UP, pp. 96—97]

That is, it was not the specific nature of Shelley's ideas so much as the intrusion of the ideas themselves, and of his own intellect, that hampered Eliot's more mature experience of reading Shelley's verse. Eliot's principle here is based on Richards's discussion of the problem of belief in Practical Criticism, which itself supports Housman's statement on the dangers of intellectualizing the poetic experience. Richards had stated in a passage quoted by Eliot:

Coleridge, when he remarked that a "willing suspension of disbe-lief" accompanied much poetry, was noting an important fact, but not quite in the happiest terms, for we are neither aware of a disbe-lief nor voluntarily suspending it in these cases. It is better to say that the question of belief or disbelief, in the intellectual sense, never arises when we are reading well. If unfortunately it does arise, either through the poet's fault or our own, we have for the moment ceased to be reading and have become astronomers, or theologians, or moralists, persons engaged in quite a different type of activity.[32]

This is a statement to which Housman could give full assent, since he defines meaning as the poem's "intellectual con-tent" (*SP*, p. 187); and I suspect that the only point of dis-agreement between Richards and Housman here would be in defining the intellect. For Richards, even the kind of reading in which the question of belief or disbelief does not arise would still, no doubt, be considered an intellectual enter-prise of some sort; for Housman, it is "more physical than intellectual" (*SP*, p. 193).

It is Housman's rigid distinction between the physical and the intellectual which leads to whatever areas of disharmony exist between his and Eliot's statements on meaning and on the nature of criticism. Although both agree that the rudimentary experience of poetry is the appeal to the read-er's sensibilities, just as "the rudiment of criticism is the ability to select a good poem and reject a bad poem" (*UP*, p. 18), Eliot adds a second step to the process: "The element of enjoyment is enlarged into appreciation, which brings a more intellectual addition to the intensity of feeling. It is a second stage in our understanding of poetry, when we no longer merely select and reject, but organise" (*UP*, p. 19). Eliot is thus uneasy with Housman's apparent attempt to rule out the intellect altogether, and, as he implies in his review of *The Name and Nature of Poetry*, his uneasiness is based in large part on his ignorance of Housman's definition of physical and intellectual.

In his concluding lecture, in the process of discussing the question of obscurity and unintelligibility, Eliot comes closest to articulating Housman's view of poetic meaning. Of the several reasons for the difficulty readers find with poetry, Eliot notes that one is the search "for a kind of 'meaning' which is not there, and is not meant to be there" (*UP*, p. 151). He states, "The chief use of the 'meaning' of a poem, in the ordinary sense, may be . . . to satisfy one habit of the reader, to keep his mind diverted and quiet, while the poem does its work upon him: much as the imaginary burglar is always provided with a nice meat for the house-dog. This is a normal situation of which I approve" (*UP*, p. 151). The analogy as well as the language of this passage suggest that meaning has little part in the real work of the poem; it is rather a necessary diversion to prevent the intrusion of the intellect and thus allow the poem (which is spoken of as something quite apart from meaning) to achieve its effect. The implication is that meaning is something unnecessary, not integral to the true experience of the poem, a view which is supported by the sentences which follow. Some poets, Eliot adds, "become impatient of this 'meaning' which seems superfluous, and perceive possibilities of intensity through its elimination. I am not asserting that this situation is ideal; only that we must write our poetry as we can, and take it as we find it" (*UP*, p. 151). Obviously an element which may be eliminated to further the intensity of the poem is not essential either to the poet's or the reader's experience of poetry, and Eliot seems as cavalier as Housman in his attitude toward meaning. He distinguishes, for example, between two types of readers—the ordinary reader, whose obsession with meaning throws him into "a state of consternation very unfavourable to poetic receptivity," and the more seasoned reader, "who has reached, in these matters, a state of greater *purity*," and who "does not bother about understanding; not, at least, at first" (*UP*, pp. 150–51). Eliot adds, of his own experience, "I know that some of the poetry to which I am most devoted is poetry which I did not understand at first reading; some is poetry which I am not sure I understand yet: for instance, Shakespeare's" (*UP*, p. 151).

Eliot's statements on meaning do not contain the heretical ring of Housman's but that may result more from a difference in temperament than from a disagreement in theory. Housman apparently savored the shock value of his rather blunt pronouncements; Eliot is constantly on guard against leaving himself open to the attack of an unfriendly critic. Eliot's eight lectures also provided him more leisure to develop and qualify his opinions. Yet taking these differences into account, it is fair to say that the status of meaning in Eliot's conception of poetry approximates that set by Housman. Eliot would not wish to assert that "meaning is of the intellect, poetry is not," but he does state that "anything that can be said as well in prose can be said better in prose," and that "a great deal, in the way of meaning, belongs to prose rather than to poetry" (*UP*, p. 152). He also adds, in the same context, that he should prefer for himself "an audience which could neither read nor write" (*UP*, p. 152). Behind both poets' statements on meaning is the assumption that poetry appeals to something in man more elementary and more primitive than the intellect; there is, in short, a depth of human feeling with which the intellect simply has nothing to do. Such an assumption is made clear in two parallel passages from the lectures. Housman, in trying to explain the effect of a line from Milton's *Arcades*, points to the non-discursive nature of poetry:

Why have the mere words the physical effect of pathos when the sense of the passage is blithe and gay? I can only say, because they are poetry, and find their way to something in man which is obscure and latent, something older than the present organisation of his nature, like the patches of fen which still linger here and there in the drained lands of Cambridgeshire. [*SP*, pp. 192–93]

Eliot's attempt to explain his own fascination with a passage in Chapman which he had twice borrowed results in a similar conclusion:

Why, for all of us, out of all that we have heard, seen, felt, in a lifetime, do certain images recur, charged with emotion, rather than others? The song of one bird, the leap of one fish, at a particular place and time, the scent of one flower, an old woman on a German mountain path, six ruffians seen through an open window playing cards at night at a small French railway junction where there was a water-mill: such memories may have symbolic value, but of what we cannot tell, for they come to represent the depths of feeling into which we cannot peer. [*UP*, p. 148]

Though Housman is referring to the images of a finished

poem and Eliot to the material that will ultimately find its way into poetry, the implication of both passages is the same. Experience, whether real or literary, makes its appeal to a region of feeling beyond the conscious mind.

This common belief in a depth of human feeling impervious to the intellect is largely responsible for the striking parallels noted here between two poets otherwise separated by taste, sensibility, and poetic technique; such a belief is most in evidence in the two poets' accounts of the creation of their own verse. Housman's almost mystical description of the composition of his verse as a passive and involuntary process characterized by illness, agitation, and exhaustion is offered as his final argument for the purely emotional nature of poetry, its nonintellectual basis. F. R. Leavis dismisses the account as the "latest notable statement" of the Romantic conception of genius and inspiration, the notion of the "essentially lyrical."[33] It is thus odd to find the poet whom Leavis had championed quoting Housman's description as confirmation of his own experience. That the two poets should have written almost identical accounts of their habits of composition only months apart is a matter of coincidence. What is significant, however, is the anti-intellectual bias which the two accounts imply. Housman takes special pains to characterize his period of creativity as "the least intellectual portion of my life" (SP, p. 194), and he describes the act of composition as pure spontaneity: "As I went along, thinking of nothing in particular . . . there would flow into my mind, with sudden and unaccountable emotion, sometimes a line or two of verse, sometimes a whole stanza at once, accompanied, not preceded, by a vague notion of the poem which they were destined to form part of " (SP, p. 194).

The same notion of spontaneity and the sense of passivity, ill-health, and anxiety characteristic of Housman's experience are so closely recalled by Eliot's account that he is careful to state in a note, "I only read Mr. Housman's essay some time after my own lines were written" (UP, p. 145n). There is a Wordsworthian ring to both accounts, but while Housman brings to mind the "spontaneous overflow" passage of the 1800 Preface, Eliot echoes the description of Wordsworth's mystical experience in "Tintern Abbey":

That there is an analogy between mystical experience and some of the ways in which poetry is written I do not deny . . . though, as I have said, whether the analogy is of significance for the student of religion, or only the psychologist, I do not know. I know, for instance, that some forms of ill-health, debility or anaemia, may (if other circumstances are favourable) produce an efflux of poetry in a way approaching the condition of automatic writing—though in contrast to the claims sometimes made for the latter, the material has obviously been incubating within the poet, and cannot be suspected of being a present from a friendly or impertinent demon. What one writes in this way may succeed in standing the examination of a more normal state of mind; it gives me the impression, as I have just said, of having undergone a long incubation, though we do not know until the shell breaks what kind of egg we have been sitting on. To me it seems that at these moments, which are characterized by the sudden lifting of the burden of anxiety and fear which presses upon our daily life so steadily that we are unaware of it, what happens is something *negative:* that is to say, not 'inspiration' as we commonly think of it, but the breaking down of strong habitual barriers—which tend to reform very quickly. Some obstruction is momentarily whisked away. The accompanying feeling is less like what we know as positive pleasure, than a sudden relief from an intolerable burden. [*UP*, pp. 144–45][34]

Eliot's references to mystical experience, automatic writing, and debility, as well as his hints of an abnormal state of mind and the presence of powers outside himself ("an outburst of words which we hardly recognise as our own," *UP*, p. 145) indicate the same nonintellectual conception of creativity that Housman reveals in other ways. Reading Eliot's account, one now understands the otherwise puzzling references in his review of Housman to "the authentic processes of a real poet" and to ill-health as a guarantee of the quality of Housman's poetry.

There is little doubt that the processes of composition recounted by Housman and Eliot played a large part in their attitudes toward the reading and criticism of poetry. Housman admits as much when he says, "My opinions on poetry are necessarily tinged, perhaps I should say tainted, by the circumstance that I have come into contact with it on two sides" (*SP*, p. 193). Eliot also notes the relationship between poetic practice and theory: "When the critics are themselves poets, it may be suspected that they have formed their critical statements with a view to justifying their poetic practice" (*UP*, p. 29). Yet in *The Use of Poetry* Eliot chooses for his models the criticism of practicing poets, and he obviously values this criticism more highly than that of critics who have viewed the process from only one side: "The critical mind operating *in* poetry, the critical effort which goes to the writing of it, may always be in advance of the critical mind operating *upon* poetry, whether it be one's own or some one else's" (*UP*, p. 30). Clearly, the passive and emotional experience of composition shared by Housman and Eliot contributed to their distrust of objective theories of criticism and to their tendency to regard meaning as of lesser importance than other components of the poetic process. The common influence in their conceptions of poetry is thus, in large part, the personal experience of writing poems rather than any shared allegiance to a specific school of criticism.

One must therefore avoid the temptation of making too much of the parallels between *The Name and Nature of Poetry* and *The Use of Poetry;* as practicing poets Eliot and Housman had little in common, and their tastes in traditional poetry were widely divergent. The critic most highly regarded by Housman and most directly responsible for his reading of the tradition of British poetry—Matthew Arnold—comes in for the harshest of Eliot's criticism in *The Use of Poetry.* Other obvious areas of disagreement might be ferreted out; yet the one thread which holds the two works together is a mutual distrust of the dominance of the intellect, a distrust which is largely responsible for the common view of the role of taste and sensibility in criticism, of the minor role of meaning in poetry, and of the major roles of passivity and spontaneity in its composition.

Of the other conclusions which may be drawn from this comparison, perhaps the most surprising is the widespread misapprehension in the thirties of Eliot's conception of poetry. Had his views been more carefully attended to, it would hardly have been possible to set him against Housman as the leader of the "intellectualist school," as Richard Aldington did, or to defend him against the implications of

Housman's lecture, as the *Scrutiny* critics did. One is led inescapably to the conclusion that what can only be called literary fashion or fad, the tendency, always present, to read a well-known poet or critic with a preconditioned response, accounted for many of the judgments of both Housman's and Eliot's criticism in the thirties. Voicing a number of the same sentiments as Housman's discredited Leslie Stephen Lecture, the Charles Eliot Norton Lectures were widely hailed, and even credited by Eliot's biographer Robert Sencourt with establishing Eliot as the leading critic of his time.[35]

The romantic and nonintellectual strain in Eliot's criticism is now somewhat easier to recognize. It has been detected principally by writers not altogether sympathetic to Eliot's critical position, most notably by Yvor Winters and Frank Kermode. Winters's essay on Eliot published in 1943 in *The Anatomy of Nonsense* was the most influential early attempt to show that the position granted Eliot as the leader of the intellectual reaction against romanticism represented a misreading of his critical views. Winters's explicit purpose was to demonstrate "that [Eliot's] intellectualism and his reactionary position are alike an illusion."[36] It is significant that his attack on Eliot centered on the very issues for which Housman was condemned. Eliot is taken to task for underestimating the value of meaning in poetry, for placing too much emphasis on the expression rather than the understanding of emotion, for believing that "the intellectual content of a poem is irrelevant to its value."[37] Kermode cites Winters's argument in *Romantic Image* (1957) to support his own view that the concept of poetry represented by Eliot's doctrine of the dissociation of sensibility is both romantic and anti-intellectual. Obviously both Winters and Kermode are pressing their own readings of twentieth-century poetry and criticism, and this is not the occasion to choose sides. Their views are mentioned here only to suggest that some modern estimates of Eliot's criticism now place him in the camp that Housman was thought to represent in 1933. In short, it is now possible to recognize that Housman has been condemned to critical oblivion for expressing a view of poetry which is not at all unlike that expressed at the same time by the most widely respected literary figure of our age.

One further response to Housman's lecture was certainly mistaken. Pound's assertion, echoed by others, that Housman was unaware of the world of his contemporaries was not true in regard to Eliot. Housman's publisher and friend Grant Richards reports that Housman kept on his shelves the works of Eliot and always spoke of his work with respect.[38] Contact between the two poets was slight. A brief correspondence between them in 1926 and 1928 concerning the works of Wilkie Collins is recorded in *The Letters of A. E. Housman*, and in 1928 Housman, in a letter to the *Times*, supplied a reading of a passage in Shelley's "To a Skylark" about which Eliot had professed ignorance in *For Lancelot Andrewes*.[39] The careers of the two poets ran in different directions, and they crossed only once, in 1933, when by chance their published lectures revealed an affinity which their contemporaries were unable to recognize and which has consequently been lost to the record of twentieth-century criticism.

*Notes*

1. "Mr. Housman at Little Bethel," p. 217.

2. "A Hope for Poetry," *Collected Poems 1929–1933* (New York: Random House, 1935), p. 162.

3. Ibid., p. 169.

4. *The Poetry of W. B. Yeats* (New York: Oxford University Press, 1941), p. 78.

5. See Louis MacNeice, *Modern Poetry* (Oxford: Clarendon Press, 1968), p. 107.

6. *Collected Shorter Poems 1927–1957* (New York: Random House, 1966). Pound's earlier "Mr. Housman's Message," published in *Canzoni* in 1911, was a less sympathetic parody:

> London is a woeful place,
> Shropshire is much pleasanter.
> Then let us smile a little space
> Upon fond nature's morbid grace.
> *Oh, Woe, woe, woe, etcetera* . . . .
>                 [ll. 11–15]

7. Quoted in D. W. Harding and L. C. Knights, "Flank-Rubbing

and Criticism," *Scrutiny* 2 (September, 1933): 183–184.

8. Quoted in Robert W. Stallman, "Annotated Bibliography of A. E. Housman: A Critical Study," *PMLA* 60 (1945): 467.

9. Quoted in Gorley Putt, "Go to the Professors!" *Scrutiny* (September, 1933): 207.

10. Ibid.

11. Ibid., pp. 207–208. The review, which considers Housman's lecture along with two other works on nineteenth-century poetry, is an implicit defense of Eliot against the claims of the Romantic tradition, which Putt interprets as "attacks on the modern 'unromantics' " (p. 208).

12. "Flank-Rubbing and Criticism," p. 183.

13. Ibid., p. 186.

14. *The Letters of A. E. Housman*, p. 344. Pound's hostile review had not yet appeared.

15. "A. E. Housman: *The Name and Nature of Poetry*," *Criterion*, 13 (October, 1933): 152.

16. Ibid.

17. In refusing permission to include his poems in A. J. A. Symons's *A Book of Nineties Verse*, Housman had said in 1928: "To include me in an anthology of the Nineties would be just as technically correct, and just as essentially inappropriate, as to include Lot in a book on Sodomites; in saying which I am not saying a word against sodomy, nor implying that intoxication and incest are in any way preferable" (*The Letters of A. E. Housman*, p. 271).

18. Eliot, p. 152.

19. Ibid., pp. 153–154.

20. Ibid., p. 154.

21. *The Use of Poetry and the Use of Criticism: Studies in the Relation of Criticism to Poetry in England* (London: Faber and Faber, 1933), p. 121. Hereafter cited in the text as *UP*.

22. The poet-critics considered by Eliot include Campion, Daniel, Sidney, Jonson, Dryden, Addison, Johnson, Wordsworth, Coleridge, Shelley, Keats, and Arnold. I. A. Richards is chosen as the representative of modern critical tendencies.

23. "The Faculty of Poets," *Virginia Quarterly Review* 10 (1934): 477, 479.

24. See "Mr. Housman at Little Bethel," p. 216.

25. Aldington, *A. E. Housman and W. B. Yeats*, p. 11.

26. "Flank-Rubbing and Criticism," p. 184.

27. Chapter 1 of *The Use of Poetry* is concluded with a long note entitled "On the Development of Taste in Poetry."

28. See *A. E. Housman and W. B. Yeats*, p. 11.

29. *The Letters of A. E. Housman*, p. 335.

30. The two quotations were aptly chosen, for both indicate the difficulty Housman acknowledges of isolating a "pure" poetic element independent of meaning. The Wordsworth passage is this:

> Sorrow, that is not sorrow, but delight;
> And miserable love, that is not pain
> To hear of, for the glory that redounds
> Therefrom to human kind, and what we are.
>                         [*Prelude* XIII, 246–249]

Emerson's "Sacrifice" depends even more heavily on the idea expressed:

> Though love repine and reason chafe,
>     There came a voice without reply,—
> ' 'Tis man's perdition to be safe,
>     When for the truth he ought to die'.

31. Eliot, pp. 153–154.

32. *Practical Criticism* (New York: Harcourt, Brace, 1929), p. 277.

33. *Revaluation* (New York: Norton, 1963), p. 208.

34. The passage from Housman which Eliot quotes as "confirmation of my own experience" is as follows: "In short, I think that the production of poetry, in its first stage, is less an active than a passive and involuntary process; and if I were obliged, not to define poetry, but to name the class of things to which it belongs, I should call it a secretion; whether a natural secretion, like turpentine in the fir, or a morbid secretion, like the pearl in the oyster. I think that my own case, though I may not deal with the material so cleverly as the oyster does, is the latter; because I have seldom written poetry unless I was rather out of health, and the experience, though pleasurable, was generally agitating and exhausting" (*SP*, p. 194).

35. *T. S. Eliot: A Memoir* (New York: Dell Publishing Co., 1971), p. 153.

36. "T. S. Eliot or The Illusion of Reaction," reprinted in *In Defense of Reason* (Denver: University of Denver Press, 1947), p. 460.

37. Ibid., p. 474.

38. *Housman 1897–1936*, pp. 337, 370.

39. See *The Letters of A. E. Housman*, pp. 227, 235, 271.

7

# BEYOND THE PLEASURE PRINCIPLE:
## The Mithridatic Function
## in Housman's Defense of Poetry

IN CONTRAST TO A POET like Eliot who cultivated the sensibilities of readers with his own criticism and theory, Housman was willing, on the whole, to allow his poems to speak for themselves. "All that need be known of my life and books," he wrote to an American scholar, "is contained in about a dozen lines of the publication *Who's Who.*"[1] His letters yield only occasional glimpses of the poet, revealing instead the reserve and fastidiousness of the scholar who seems more concerned with printers' errors than with the substance of his poems. His published prose[2] is likewise devoted primarily to the concerns of the classical scholar, and *The Name and Nature of Poetry* remains his one comprehensive statement on the art of poetry. Only one other source of information on Housman's poetics rivals the lecture in interest, and that is the poetry itself.

It is not surprising, given Housman's reticence, that he should have chosen his verse as the mode for the expression of a defense of his own poetry. The pastoral mask, Terence, had become, after all, a means of dealing with feeling and experiences beyond or below the range exhibited by the reserved bachelor. It is fitting, therefore, that while Housman delivered his public lecture on poetry in the person of the scientist-scholar, his private thoughts on the subject were given more than thirty years earlier by Terence Hearsay in the concluding two poems of *A Shropshire Lad.* Of the two,

113

"Terence, this is stupid stuff" is the more important for an understanding of Housman's conception of the nature of his own poetry. The concluding poem, "I hoed and trenched and weeded," offers a rather conventional view of the permanence of art in contrast to the mutability of the artist, but "Terence" develops a striking and significant theory of art.

The conceptions of poetry articulated in "Terence" and *The Name and Nature of Poetry* were published at the opposite ends of Housman's career, the first in 1896, the second in 1933, three years before his death. Yet they are not two separate theories; the differences in them are the obvious differences of mode, intent, and emphasis. While the lecture is general and comprehensive, scholarly in tone, composed for a university audience, the earlier work is specific, personal in tone, and characterized by the pastoral mode that informs the whole of *A Shropshire Lad*. The primary difference is, however, to be seen in the divergent aims of the two works. In the Leslie Stephen Lecture Housman attempts to define the very essence of poetry, all poetry, to isolate the one element which separates poetry from all other species of writing. In "Terence" he is primarily interested in his own poetry, and in only one aspect of that—the despondent and pessimistic nature of his verse, its painful effect on the reader. The general aesthetic issue which Housman considers in "Terence" is one that has interested theorists since Aristotle. Stated simply, it is this: how can an art which deals with the unpleasant and the painful bring pleasure, or some corresponding benefit, to its audience? In "Terence," Housman contrives the situation in which the question can be asked and answered, and though his answer seems directed specifically to the qualities of his own poetry, it is not limited to that, as may be seen in looking at two other classic statements of the issue he considers.

The tragic pleasure, Aristotle had said, is that of pity and fear, and he had noted that objects which in life would bring pain or disgust may be viewed with pleasure if reproduced, however realistically, in art.[3] Housman's own favorite critic Matthew Arnold had also pondered this seemingly paradoxical issue, and, like Housman, he had done so in relation to his own poetry. Arnold states in the "Preface to *Poems*

(1853)": "In presence of the most tragic circumstances, represented in a work of Art, the feeling of enjoyment, as is well known, may still subsist: the representation of the most utter calamity, of the liveliest anguish, is not sufficient to destroy it: the more tragic the situation, the deeper becomes the enjoyment; and the situation is more tragic in proportion as it becomes more terrible."[4]

Both Aristotle and Arnold offer explanations for this phenomenon which I wish to consider in relation to Housman's own theory, and I quote them primarily as a means of demonstrating Housman's divergence from the established conceptions of the relationship of artistic pleasure and real pain. Aristotle's explanation (or at least one of them) is found in man's delight in imitation: "Imitation is natural to man from childhood, one of his advantages over the lower animals being this, that he is the most imitative creature in the world, and learns at first by imitation. And it is also natural for all to delight in works of imitation."[5] The more influential explanation for the pleasure man experiences in viewing painful events is found in Aristotle's concept of catharsis. He does not, unfortunately, elaborate on the concept at any length; he speaks simply of the work containing "incidents arousing pity and fear, wherewith to accomplish its catharsis of such emotions."[6] Consequently, no word employed in the *Poetics* has occasioned more disagreement. The conventional interpretation has, however, been seen in terms of a pleasurable release of the fear and anxiety excited by the tragedy, an emotional outlet which cleanses the audience of the harmful effects of the feelings which the work itself produced. Although that is to put it somewhat too simply, Aristotle is traditionally seen as providing at least two explanations for the artistic transformation of pain into pleasure—mimesis and catharsis.

Arnold extends the issue a step further. He agrees that we take pleasure in imitation or representation, "inasmuch as it gratifies this natural interest in knowledge of all kinds,"[7] yet he makes a more specific demand of the poet:

Any accurate representation may therefore be expected to be interesting; but, if the representation be a poetical one, more than this is demanded. It is demanded not only that it shall interest, but also that it shall inspirit and rejoice the reader: that it shall convey a charm, and infuse delight. . . . it is not enough that the Poet should add to the knowledge of men, it is required of him also that he should add to their happiness.[8]

Imitation in itself is thus not a sufficient justification for a poetical work; it must also be a representation from which men can derive enjoyment. In locating the element which provides such enjoyment, Arnold arrives at a concept somewhat analogous to Aristotle's catharsis:

What then are the situations, from the representation of which, though accurate, no poetical enjoyment can be derived? They are those in which the suffering finds no vent in action; in which a continuous state of mental distress is prolonged, unrelieved by incident, hope or resistance; in which there is everything to be endured, nothing to be done. In such situations there is inevitably something morbid, in the description of them something monotonous. When they occur in actual life, they are painful, not tragic; the representation of them in poetry is painful also.[9]

Arnold makes an additional demand of the poet which is not contained in Aristotle—that the work itself offer some positive element which will relieve the state of mental distress and "inspirit and rejoice the reader." His concept of suffering finding vent in action is not altogether clear and presents problems in describing his theory, yet it seems to accomplish the same general function as Aristotle's idea of catharsis; in both cases the emotions generated by the work find release—either in the audience, according to Aristotle's formulation,[10] or in the work itself (if I read him correctly) according to Arnold's. When we turn to Housman's treatment of this issue in "Terence," we discover a justification for the painful nature of art which is neither strictly Greek nor Victorian. Although it contains some mimetic elements, it does not seek relief from pain by catharsis or action. Housman formulates instead a notion by which poetry becomes a defense not through release from pain but through acceptance of it.

The poem's position at the conclusion of *A Shropshire Lad* and its use of the persona Terence as the poet (for the first time in the volume) lend support to the idea that Housman is using "Terence" as a means of justifying the theme and tone of the poems which precede it.[11] The seriousness of his intent is somewhat disguised by the witty and comic form the poem assumes, but that in itself becomes one of the means of defense. The form of the poem is quite simple. In the first fourteen lines Housman creates a comic adversary who voices the issue confronted by Aristotle and Arnold. In the remaining sixty-two lines, Housman, through Terence, offers a concept of poetry which justifies the pain and anxiety occasioned by his verse and presents a model (in the tale of Mithridates) for his view of the painful relationship of art and life. The poem, one of Housman's more frequently anthologized, is now so well known that a paraphrase is hardly necessary. However, to see the issues the poem raises in the critical context I have been discussing, it is useful to translate its comic exaggerations into a more commonplace idiom.

Housman's critic begins with the implication that Terence's poetry is so despondent as to suggest that he is suffering from some illness, although he shows no other symptoms (ll. 1–4). More important, however, is the notion that the painful and pessimistic nature of his poetry is actually transmitted to the reader. It brings real pain ("gives a chap the belly-ache," l. 6),[12] but also contributes despondency, melancholy, even madness (l. 13). Terence's poetry is seen as a kind of disease which has infected the poet, "killed the cow" (l. 10), and now threatens to send his "friends to death before their time" (l. 12). The unrelieved misery of the poetry seems to correspond roughly to the kind of verse Arnold sought to exclude from the poetic canon,[13] that is, a poetry "in which a continuous state of mental distress is prolonged, unrelieved by incident, hope or resistance." Such verse, says Arnold, is merely painful, not noble or tragic. Yet where Arnold asks for action to vent the suffering, Terence's critic asks for something light and happy, "a tune to dance to" (l. 14).

Having played the critic, Housman, through the persona of Terence, now assumes the role of the poet who must defend himself against the charge that his verse brings not pleasure but pain. His argument, in brief summary, is that the painful view of life contained in his poetry best serves as a defense against the much harsher pain of life itself. Since the world has "much less good than ill" (l. 44), the wise man should "train for ill and not for good" (l. 48). Terence's poetry, in the metaphor of drink which controls the poem, is both painful and sour, but ultimately of more value than attempts to escape the reality of life's ills:

> 'Tis true, the stuff I bring for sale
> Is not so brisk a brew as ale:
> Out of a stem that scored the hand
> I wrung it in a weary land.
> But take it: if the smack is sour,
> The better for the embittered hour;
> It should do good to heart and head
> When your soul is in my soul's stead;
> And I will friend you, if I may,
> In the dark and cloudy day.
>                                    [ll. 49–58]

Attempts to evade or escape the unpleasant reality of life, on the other hand, are doomed to failure. A pleasurable illusion such as drinking, which leads one "To see the world as the world's not" (l. 26), is transitory and can only return one to the old world again to "begin the game anew" (l. 42). The proper model for Housman's reader is thus Mithridates, who acquired immunity from the greater poison of life by taking smaller daily doses:

> He gathered all that springs to birth
> From the many-venomed earth;
> First a little, thence to more,
> He sampled all her killing store;
> And easy, smiling, seasoned sound,
> Sate the king when healths went round. . . .
> —I tell the tale that I heard told.
> Mithridates, he died old.
>                                    [ll. 63–68, 75–76]

Such is the statement of the poem in summary and, thus simplified, not particularly promising or convincing as a theory of the relationship of art and life. It has never been taken seriously, but then its lighthearted tone has worked against it, and the very fact that it is a poem, not a lecture or an essay, has conditioned its reception. Yet one cannot dismiss the concept merely because of its poetic form; to do so would be to throw out such important statements as, say, Stevens's *Notes Toward a Supreme Fiction,* to mention only one obvious example. The comic tone can also be defended, and my overly simplified paraphrase, which fails to do justice to the subtleties of both statement and form, requires further clarification. Yet at this point it is clear that Housman's concept signals something of a departure from the line of development represented by Aristotle and Arnold since it makes no attempt to relieve the audience of the pain and anxiety generated by the work, requiring instead that the reader accept the pain as a necessary "training" or defense against the greater pain of life. To locate a modern analogue to Housman's concept, one must turn from the poets to the psychoanalytic theory of Freud. It is curious that the theory contained in "Terence" should have been so totally ignored since it anticipates by more than twenty years an idea developed by Freud which Lionel Trilling has said is as important as anything else that Freud contributed to literature.[14] I am referring to the theory advanced in Freud's *Beyond the Pleasure Principle.*

Freud's essay, published in 1920, was prompted by his discovery of certain facts which were at variance with his earlier formulation of the pleasure principle, according to which dreams could be seen as fulfilling the dreamer's desires. In Freud's earlier theory, all fantasies, including the artist's fantasies, could be explained as operating according to a hedonistic principle. Freud had used this theory to explain the pleasure the reader derives from a work of literature. In "Writers and Day-Dreaming" (1908) Freud, equating poetry with fantasy, concluded that the pleasure we derive from the literary work is at the level of fantasy, which the writer has made accessible to us through the "secret" of his art:

When a creative writer presents his plays to us or tells us what we are inclined to take to be his personal daydreams, we experience a great pleasure, and one which probably arises from the confluence of many sources. How the writer accomplishes this is his innermost secret; the essential *ars poetica* lies in the technique of overcoming the feeling of repulsion in us which is undoubtedly connected with the barriers that rise between each single ego and the others. We can guess two of the methods used by this technique. The writer softens the character of his egoistic daydreams by altering and disguising it, and he bribes us by the purely formal—that is, aesthetic—yield of pleasure which he offers us in the presentation of his phantasies. We give the name of an *incentive bonus*, or a *fore-pleasure*, to a yield of pleasure such as this, which is offered to us so as to make possible the release of still greater pleasure arising from deeper psychical sources. In my opinion, all the aesthetic pleasure which a creative writer affords us has the character of a fore-pleasure of this kind, and our actual enjoyment of an imaginative work proceeds from a liberation of tensions in our minds.[15]

In *Beyond the Pleasure Principle*, however, Freud was forced to revise his theory of dreams, although he did not extend the revisions to his theory of aesthetic pleasure. Two types of cases had presented themselves which cast doubt on the universal application of the pleasure principle in the interpretation of dreams or fantasies. In the case of war neuroses, the patient's recurring dreams returned him to the terrifying situation which produced his suffering when, according to the wish-fulfillment theory, he should have avoided this terror, dreaming instead of his healthy past or the cure he hoped to achieve. Observation of the play of children revealed a similar phenomenon in that children's games were frequently based on the most frightening and unpleasant of the child's experiences. To account for these deviations from his earlier concept, Freud developed a new theory which he at first put forward only as speculation but which, according to his editor and translator James Strachey, may be regarded as introducing the final phase of his views, presenting a new picture of the structure of the mind which was to dominate all of his later writings.[16]

Freud postulates, in brief, that there exists in the mind a compulsion to repeat which is prior to the pleasure principle, "something that seems more primitive, more elementary, more instinctual than the pleasure principle which it over-rides."[17] The function of this compulsion to repeat is actually to develop anxiety or fear by which to master the overpowering stimulus which was the cause of the original anxiety:

It is not in the service of [the pleasure] principle that the dreams of patients suffering from traumatic neuroses lead them back with such regularity to the situation in which the trauma occurred. We may assume, rather, that dreams are here helping to carry out another task, which must be accomplished before the dominance of the pleasure principle can even begin. These dreams are endeavouring to master the stimulus retrospectively, by developing the anxiety whose omission was the cause of the traumatic neurosis.[18]

Similarly, in the play of children the compulsion to repeat unhappy and threatening experiences, Freud theorizes, serves a defensive function: "children repeat unpleasurable experiences for the additional reason that they can master a powerful impression far more thoroughly by being active than they could by merely experiencing it passively. Each fresh repetition seems to strengthen the mastery they are in search of."[19] Such a compulsion to repeat painful experiences for the purpose of mastery is not confined, in his view, to shell-shocked patients and children but is a part of a larger instinctual pattern, a pattern which leads Freud, in the same essay, to the postulation of a universal death-wish.[20]

This detour into Freud's metapsychology may appear to have taken us away from the aesthetic issues with which we began, but, in fact, it brings us closer to an appreciation of Housman's attempt to resolve an age-old critical problem—the fascination of both artist and audience in that which produces anxiety and pain. In *Beyond the Pleasure Principle*, Freud speculates that there is a human need which is more elementary than pleasure, a compulsion to defend against the pain of life by deliberately creating anxiety-producing experiences through fantasy or play for the purpose of mastery. This is, of course, the basis of Housman's defense in "Terence" of his own painful poetry. Lionel Trilling's description in *The Liberal Imagination* of Freud's theory is, in this regard, a most accurate account of Housman's own theory, although he does not mention Housman. Trilling speaks of "the mind embracing its own pain for some vital purpose," and of "the homeopathic administration of pain to inure ourselves to the greater pain which life will force upon us." Most significantly, he calls this theory in Freud "the mithridatic function,"[21] although he fails to note that Housman had anticipated this theory, complete with Mithridates, by a quarter of a century.

It would be futile (and beside the point) to argue that Housman's poetic expression parallels Freud's theory exactly or to insist that there was any link between the two. Although Freud gave credit for his discoveries to the poets and philosophers who preceded him, stating that it would be "difficult to escape what is universally known,"[22] Housman simply presented the aesthetic equivalent of Freud's later metapsychological theory. This in itself presents a complication, however, since Freud was unwilling to apply the insights of *Beyond the Pleasure Principle* to aesthetics.

Freud tended to rely on Aristotle in his attempts to account for the fact that "many excitements which, in themselves, are actually distressing, can become a source of pleasure for the hearers and spectators at the performance of a writer's work."[23] In "Psychopathic Characters on the Stage," written in 1904 but not published until 1942, he clearly employs Aristotle's notion of catharsis translated into his own psychoanalytical terms:

> If the function of the drama, as has been assumed since Aristotle, is to excite pity and fear, and thus bring about a 'catharsis of the emotions', we may describe this same purpose a little more fully if we say that the question is one of opening up sources of pleasure and enjoyment from within the sphere of the intellect, through the action of which many such sources had been made inaccessible. Certainly the release of the subject's own affects must here be given first place, and the enjoyment resulting therefrom corresponds on the one hand to the relief produced by their free discharge, and on the other, very likely, to the concommitant sexual stimulation which, one may suppose, occurs as a by-product of every emotional excitation and supplies the subject with that feeling of a heightening of his psychic level which he so greatly prizes.[24]

Freud suggests further that the witnessing of a dramatic performance fulfills the same gratification for the adult as play does for the child. The pleasure derived presupposes an illusion. The viewer is given the opportunity to identify himself with a hero and to participate in his painful experiences yet is spared real suffering through his knowledge, first, that it is not actually he who suffers on the stage, and, second, that it is only a play, therefore no threat to his personal security.[25]

Aristotle's concept of catharsis was thus congenial to Freud early in his career because it offered an explanation that was not a violation of the pleasure principle for the viewer's attraction to the painful. By 1920, however, Freud was prepared to go beyond the pleasure principle, and his speculations on the compulsion to repeat led him back to the problem of artistic suffering. Curiously, however, he does not alter his earlier Aristotelian view of tragedy. Freud notes the obvious parallel between the play of children which repeats unpleasurable experience and the artistic play of adults which serves the same function. Yet he maintains his original concept that the latter operates according to the pleasure principle and requires no further explanation: "The artistic play and artistic imitation carried out by adults, which, unlike children's, are aimed at an audience, do not spare the spectators (for instance, in tragedy) the most painful experiences and can yet be felt by them as highly enjoyable."[26] He regards this assumption that tragedy is indeed enjoyable to the spectators as "convincing proof" that even under the pleasure principle there are means of making what is in itself unpleasant a source of pleasure, and he considers the problem presented by artistic depictions of suffering to lie outside the area of experience suggested by the compulsion to repeat:

The consideration of these cases and situations, which have a yield of pleasure as their final outcome, should be undertaken by some system of aesthetics with an economic approach to its subject-matter. They are of no use for our purpose, since they presuppose the existence and dominance of the pleasure principle; they give no evidence of the operation of tendencies *beyond* the pleasure principle, that is, of tendencies more primitive than it and independent of it.[27]

Freud's willingness to exclude literary depictions of pain from the newer speculations of *Beyond the Pleasure Principle* is obviously based on his assumption that enjoyment or pleasure is the proper characterization of the aesthetic experience of tragedy. He does not consider the possibility, suggested by theories like Housman's, that pleasure, even in

the broad sense used by Freud, is not the most apt term for
many subjective responses to literature. But even if the pleasure principle offers a satisfactory explanation for some or
most of the elements of the audience's response to painful
literature, that does not rule out the possibility of other
equally satisfactory explanations or of the presence of
psychological responses in addition to the hedonistic one
associated with catharsis. Freud located the compulsion to
return to anxiety-producing situations in the play of children and in dreams, and, significantly, he noted earlier that
the sympathetic witnessing of a dramatic performance fulfills the same function for the adult as does play for the
child[28] and that the creative writer is merely the "dreamer
in broad daylight."[29]

Moreover, Freud's formulation of a compulsion more ele-
mental than the pleasure principle has been seen by later
critics as holding greater promise for the study of tragic or
painful art than he was willing to allow. In "Freud and Literature," Trilling states:

[Freud] does not wish to believe that this effort to come to mental
grips with a situation is involved in the attraction of tragedy. He is,
we might say, under the influence of the Aristotelian tragic theory
which emphasizes a qualified hedonism through suffering. But the
pleasure involved in tragedy is perhaps an ambiguous one; and
sometimes we must feel that the famous sense of cathartic resolution is perhaps the result of glossing over terror with beautiful
language rather than an evacuation of it. And sometimes the terror
even bursts through the language to stand stark and isolated from
the play as does Oedipus's sightless and bleeding face.[30]

And Trilling concludes, in a statement to which I have already referred, that the Aristotelian concept does not rule
out the possibility that tragedy as well as other forms of
literature may serve functions other than hedonistic ones:

The Aristotelian theory does not deny another function for tragedy
(and for comedy, too) which is suggested by Freud's theory of the
traumatic neurosis—what might be called the mithridatic function,
by which tragedy is used as the homeopathic administration of pain
to inure ourselves to the greater pain which life will force upon us.
There is in the cathartic theory of tragedy, as it is usually understood, a conception of tragedy's function which is too negative and

which inadequately suggests the sense of active mastery which tragedy can give.[31]

With the concepts of the "homeopathic administration of pain" and "active mastery" we are back, finally, to Housman's concept of painful poetry in "Terence," but now, I hope, with some perspective on the larger issue Housman was addressing. I have attempted thus far to establish the legitimacy of Housman's concept of poetry in "Terence" and to relate it to other formulations directed to the same critical problem. In doing so, however, I have treated "Terence" as if it were merely a statement, not a poem, and that is, of course, somewhat misleading. To understand fully the implications of Housman's treatment of the art of poetry in "Terence" it is necessary to take into account the form of the poem as well. Furthermore, both the theme and the form of the poem may be more clearly articulated when examined in the light of some modern formulations of the Freudian theory I have been discussing.

Modern psychoanalytic critics such as Ernst Kris, Norman Holland, and Simon O. Lesser have extended Freud's theories of art by emphasizing the concepts of mastery and defense to a greater extent than Freud was willing to do. The result has been to bring these modern Freudian theories closer to Housman's idea, even if they are still not identical in every respect. Although Housman's Terence argues that there is a satisfaction to be found in the mastery provided by his despondent and melancholy poetry, his friend's reaction to that poetry, voiced in the first fourteen lines of the poem, implies that pleasure is not an appropriate term for his response. Yet contemporary Freudian critics tend to identify the sense of mastery provided by painful literature as one of the reader's sources of pleasure. Ernst Kris, for example, refers to "functional" pleasure observed both in children's play and in literary response, which he defines as "pleasure arising from a sense of mastery" by overcoming "the outer world and anxiety."[32] In extending Freud's concept of catharsis, Kris states:

The progress of psychoanalytical knowledge has opened the way for a better understanding of the cathartic effect; we are no longer satisfied with the notion that repressed emotions lose their hold over our mental life when an outlet for them has been found. We believe rather that what Aristotle describes as the purging enables the ego to reestablish the control which is threatened by dammed-up instinctual demands. The search for outlets acts as an aid to assuring or reestablishing this control, and the pleasure is a double one, in both discharge and control.[33]

Norman Holland also locates one of the sources of pleasure which painful literature provides in its defensive strategy. After considering the theories of Aristotle and Arnold concerning the problem of tragic suffering, he concludes:

The psychoanalytic critic can generalize Arnold's and Aristotle's disparate explanations into the single notion of defensive management, but the question as to how a defense can reverse pain into pleasure reaches to the edges of psychoanalytic knowledge. My sketchy and empirical observations on literary affect seem to suggest that affect can arise as a kind of by-product from the application (by the literary work) of a certain kind of defensive maneuver. Denial can turn anxiety into reassurance. If so, then we would have to think in terms of two separate sources for affect: one the fantasy, the other the defense. Which dominates would depend on their relative strengths.[34]

Holland, following Simon O. Lesser, thus locates two sources of aesthetic pleasure, one in the gratification of desires, the other in the defense against or mastery of anxiety and pain. These two pleasures correspond in a rough way to the division of content and form; as Lesser puts it, "It seems probable that our desires are chiefly—not, of course, exclusively—satisfied by subject matter, our defenses by form."[35]

Clearly, then, the "functional" pleasure of Kris, that is, the pleasure derived from a sense of mastery, and the concepts of form as defensive mastery in Lesser and Holland are the modern psychoanalytic equivalents of Housman's mithridatic principle. The clearest statement of this principle in contemporary Freudian theory is found in Lesser's treatment of fiction. Our eagerness to read fiction which refuses to gloss over painful experiences, Lesser argues, may be traced to the same impulses which Freud found in the traumatic neuroses: "A person may return again and again to an event which caused him suffering and go over it in his mind and feelings until he has assimilated its pain and regained his stability." By an extension of this idea, Lesser finds, people turn to art and play to master not only past causes of anxiety but possible future cases as well. Art enables them "to deal in imagination with any situation which might cause pain, and thus strengthen their ability to cope with it."[36] Like Housman, Lesser finds the proper model for this theory in the tale of Mithridates: "In very much the same fashion in which Mithridates' small doses of poison prepared him to tolerate the prescriptions of his enemies, the fictional encounter with anxiety, weathered, fortifies us for dealing with whatever perils the future holds. It gives us a feeling of being able to shoulder far heavier burdens than we have thus far been asked to assume, and the ones we have been carrying by comparison now seem light."[37]

Also like Housman, Lesser is hesitant to label this mithridatic function of art as pleasure, and his attempt to describe the effect of such art is instructive:

We are impelled to project ourselves into such fiction as this, I believe, not so much by the hope of pleasure as by the desire to secure relief and a measure of immunity from pain. . . . So far as I know there is no exact word in the language for what we feel. A subdued exhilaration—that is the best approximation I can achieve for the element which predominates. We may also experience a sense of strength and a feeling of quiet pride. The exhilaration is muffled because it seems unjustified and, as it were, illogical; it is qualified by a continuing sense of the seriousness and painfulness of the human situation.[38]

This distinction is important, I believe, because the tendency of Freud and his followers has been to secure the domain of art under the agency of the pleasure principle through a modification of Aristotle's catharsis (as with Freud), a concept such as Kris's "functional" pleasure, or Holland's theory that the defensive strategies of literature are themselves sources of pleasure. However, both Housman and Lesser seem willing to qualify the notion of pleasure with the addition of a concept of small doses of pain. Lesser expresses this idea quite explicitly in regard to fiction:

Essentially, great fiction relieves anxiety by helping us to confront and work through the conflicts which arouse anxiety and our anxieties themselves. It permits us to do this in large part unconsciously, and in a dozen other ways seeks to minimize the painfulness of the experience. But it neither denies nor disparages the seriousness of the issues with which it deals; it does not attempt to eliminate pain. Rather, it requires that we temporarily experience a certain amount of anxiety, just as a vaccination gives us a small and controlled case of the disease it is meant to prevent.[39]

Although Lesser's theory of immunization is the only one of these three modern psychoanalytic theories that parallels Housman's formulation exactly, Holland's extension of the concepts of Kris and Lesser into the analysis of poetic style is also of great value in a description of Housman's idea of painful art in "Terence." Holland has provided a model for the analysis of the kind of defensive mastery which Housman claimed poetry provides, and in such instances as his well-known analysis of "Dover Beach" he has demonstrated how the purely formal devices of a poem may serve to modify defensively its content.[40] A cursory reading of "Terence" might indicate that it is only in the painful subject matter of poetry that the mithridatic function is to be found, but an examination of the formal elements of the poem makes clear what Holland has noted—that form plays an even greater role in defensive mastery than the paraphrasable content. I am not prepared to subject "Terence" to the sort of psychoanalytic analysis meant to uncover the unconscious fantasy level of the poem, but I am interested in the means by which the poem's form handles its intellectual content, especially since these formal elements provide additional insights into Housman's conception of what I have been calling the mithridatic function of poetry.[41]

A traditional psychoanalytic view is that we come to a literary work with at least two conscious expectations: "First, that it will give us pleasure (of an oral, 'taking in' kind); second, that it will not require us to act on the external world."[42] It is interesting to note how the formal devices of Housman's "Terence" manipulate these expectations and, indeed, deny their validity. That is, the imagery, structure, and tone of the poem clearly reinforce and extend the mithridatic principle contained in its intellectual content.

   The imagery is almost exactly what we might anticipate in
a poem dealing with the writing and reading of poetry. It is
predominantly of an oral, "taking in" kind, fulfilling the
expectations of psychoanalytic criticism, which has noted
the close correlation between oral experience—eating and
drinking—and aesthetic experience.[43] Imagery of food and
drink closely associated with the writing of poetry is intro-
duced from almost the first line:

> 'Terence, this is stupid stuff:
> You eat your victuals fast enough;
> There can't be much amiss, 'tis clear,
> To see the rate you drink your beer.
> But oh, good Lord, the verse you make,
> It gives a chap the belly-ache.'
>
> [ll. 1–6]

The pattern of imagery reverses the traditional pleasurable
associations between poetry and eating (or drinking), since
the "stuff" that Terence makes produces not pleasure but
pain, a stomachache. This reversal of the reader's pleasurable expectation is continued throughout the poem as Terence picks up the drinking-poetry metaphor contained in his
friend's objection to his verse and expands it in a number of
different ways. He first compares his poetry, seen as strong
drink, to real liquor (ll. 15–42), then justifies the unpleasant
nature of his verse by developing the metaphor of poetry as a
bitter drink which is "not so brisk a brew as ale" (l. 50). It has
painful consequences both for the poet and the reader—for
the poet because it is wrung from a thorny stem that "scored
the hand" (l. 51), for the reader because it is "sour," hard to
take. Of course its justification lies precisely in its medicinal
value, suggested by the punning phrase "take it" (which
carries both the meaning of bear it and ingest it, as in "taking" medicine) and by the bitter taste:

> But take it: if the smack is sour,
> The better for the embittered hour;
> It should do good to heart and head
> When your soul is in my soul's stead;
> And I will friend you, if I may,
> In the dark and cloudy day.
>
> [ll. 53–58]

Finally, the food-poetry parallel is transmuted into Mithridates's "poisoned meat and poisoned drink" (l. 62), and the bitter drink metaphor is extended a step further, the medicinal implications of the earlier imagery having developed into the notion of immunization.[44] The imagery of the Mithridates passage suggests that painful poetry is not simply sour or bitter, but a smaller dose of the very thing it defends against. Here life is seen as a poisoned feast, poetry as a product of the "many-venomed earth." The reader samples "First a little, thence to more" until he has mastered "all her killing store" and is immune from the "arsenic in his meat" and the "strychnine in his cup" (quotations from ll. 60–71). In brief, the imagery introduces the traditional concept of the reader's expectation that poetry will provide pleasure (of an oral, "taking in" kind), implies that this is an illusion comparable to the state of intoxication, then presents a concept of poetry as first a sour medicine and, finally, as a controlled dose of poison.

This conflict between pleasure and pain is reinforced and complicated by a further conflict between illusion and reality, hinted at above, which brings us to the second of the reader's expectations—that poetry "will not require us to act on the external world." Clearly this expectation is contained in Terence's friend's injunction that he substitute for his despondent poetry "a tune to dance to," that is, something sunny and light which will gloss over the unpleasant aspects of experience on which Terence's poetry is based. To counter this expectation, the poem merges the imagery of drink with images suggesting a contrast between games and real life, intoxication and sobriety, lies and truth—that is, attempts to escape the painful nature of life as against the willingness to face up to it. The desire of the reader to separate art from life and to regard art as an escape or temporary diversion from anxiety is developed primarily by images of intoxication and play. Since it "hurts to think" (l. 23), dancing and drinking offer pleasant alternatives, but they have two serious drawbacks—they are illusory and they are temporary:

> Look into the pewter pot
> To see the world as the world's not.

And faith, 'tis pleasant till 'tis past:
The mischief is that 'twill not last.
[ll. 25–28]

Pleasurable images are here associated with illusion, painful ones with reality—the "lovely muck" of a drunken sleep when "the world seemed none so bad," the "tale" which is "all a lie," the "game" which must be begun anew after each escape, as opposed to the world at waking the morning after: "The world, it was the old world yet, / I was I, my things were wet" (quotations from ll. 33–42). The pleasant illusions—tales, games, lies, dancing, drunkenness—are by implication equated with the sort of escapist poetry which Terence's critic requests, and the function of the imagery is not only to develop an illusion-reality contrast but also to place Terence's poetry on the side of reality. In short, Housman answers the reader's desire for a poetry unrelated to reality by noting that such a poetry leads one to falsify experience and to obtain only temporary relief from anxiety.

If this seems to be no more than a self-serving answer to a legitimate complaint against the kind of poetry that Housman wrote, it may be compared to a statement on the same issue by Lesser in regard to fiction. Lesser, like Housman, finds that many readers want an immediate respite from anxiety—"a narcotic which will enable them to forget the painful aspects of experience and their own troublesome drives and conflicts." However, he notes, such literature succeeds only by falsifying experience: "When such determinedly sunny fiction is successful, it does offer a haven from anxiety. Unfortunately, to create such a haven, fiction must usually sidestep adult concerns and falsify the issues with which it deals. It is nearly always compelled to resort to some degree of falsification to make the issues susceptible to easy and happy solution."[45] Furthermore, Lesser concludes as Housman did that the relief offered by a literature which glosses over the real problems of life is only temporary:

Obviously, the kind of fiction of which I am speaking can comfort only those people who are blind to its shortcomings or so desperate for an anodyne they are willing to disregard them. Even the relief it offers such readers is ephemeral in the extreme. It may even be succeeded, as soon as they put down their novel or magazine, or walk out of the movie palace into the night, by a feeling of having been deceived. In any case the euphoria quickly vanishes. There is no carryover relief or satisfaction of the kind we so often experience after reading serious fiction, no sense of understanding more or being better fortified to cope with one's problems.[46]

Lesser's parallel statement on "serious" fiction, I believe, lends some authority to the attitude expressed by Housman that literature, far from separating us from the real world, returns us to reality fortified against it.

It is true that we recognize literature as a "fiction" of some order, but that does not deny the implication of Housman's notion that literature is not an escape from but a confrontation with reality.[47] The illusion-reality conflict suggested in the imagery of "Terence" is developed further in the poem's structure, and it is significant that the structural elements both of "Terence" itself and of *A Shropshire Lad* as a whole work to move us from a sense of illusion to one of reality. Holland, in discussing our conscious expectations in experiencing literature (that the work will please us and that we will not have to act on it), notes that the frustration of either expectation can lead to some of the more exotic effects possible in art. He mentions, for example, novels like *Tristram Shandy* which are "novels about writing the novel which is the novel." And he finds that such effects are "unsettling," since they "create an uncertainty in us as to whether the supposed fiction we are reading or watching is really a fiction or a reality about a fiction."[48] Housman creates such an effect in "Terence," and it serves to reinforce the poem's statement that a function of art is to provide small doses of reality, not escapist fantasies.

"Terence" is built on a two-part structure—the critic's attack and the poet's answer. It is, in short, a poem about a poet answering a review of his poetry, and it poses the question of the relationship of the poem we are reading to the poetry he is defending. Furthermore, the form of the poet's defense of his poetry is itself a poem in the manner of the poetry which is being criticized. This strategy creates an intellectual maze, and the result is to juggle our conventional sense of illusion and reality. Holland notes in regard to such a structure, "Because these effects make me uncertain as to whether I am confronting a reality or a fiction, something to be or not to be introjected in a primitive way, I find my own position in reality called into question.''[49] The issue is further complicated by the position of the poem at the conclusion of a volume of lyrics. In *A Shropshire Lad* we have read the poems of the fictional persona Terence; now Terence appears to defend these very poems. This establishes a different order of fiction (or reality) for the poem in which the poet himself appears (although Terence is himself a fiction with Housman the poet still lurking behind him). If the other poems were fictions, then this poem which discusses them cannot be a fiction on exactly the same level. If, in the concluding chapter of a novel, the supposed author of the novel appeared to defend the theme and tone of the work we were still reading, it would produce the same unsettling effect. What precisely that effect is in "Terence" is difficult to say. Although we may not feel that the poem is "real," we certainly sense that it is more in touch with reality than the preceding poems precisely because it encompasses them. At the very least, this strategy makes us consciously aware of the intrusion of reality into art, the effect that Housman requires in a poem that argues that poetry should not escape from the real.

If I am correct in my analysis, then, the imagery and structure of "Terence" serve to deny two of the most widely held beliefs about poetry—that its function is to provide pleasure and that it does not require us to interact with the real world. There is, however, a third aspect of the poem's style which must be taken into account, its comic tone. We are confronted with a string of ironies. It seems odd that Housman would defend the despondent nature of his poetry with light verse (which amounts almost to giving in to his critic). Further, the comic tone appears to be at odds with the theme that poetry is a serious business. Finally, we are told that Terence's poetry is painful and sour, yet the form of the poem itself gives little evidence of that. The language is hardly tragic or even bitter, consisting of such phrases as "stupid stuff," "belly-ache," "such tunes as killed the cow," "lovely muck." There is also the famous put-down of Milton (or God): "malt does more than Milton can / To justify God's

ways to man" (ll. 21–22), and an extended playful description
of the effects of drink ("Oh I have been to Ludlow fair / And
left my necktie God knows where," ll. 29–30). The Mithridates passage also contains several punning references to
eating and health ("And easy, smiling, seasoned sound, /
Sate the king when healths went round," ll. 67–68). Clearly,
this comic tone is characteristic of the speaker's voice
throughout the poem. So how are we to account for an apparent discrepancy between theme and style? More important, how is the comic manner related to the mithridatic
function of art which the poem proposes?

The answer to both questions is to be found, I believe, in
one aspect of Housman's defense which I have not emphasized to this point. Since Housman argues, in effect, that
his poetry benefits the reader by giving him doses of the
actual pain and anxiety of the real world, the reader might
well respond that this sort of poetry is unnecessary since it
provides in a haphazard way what reality does much better.
The answer to this objection is that art, unlike reality, can
provide the pain and anxiety in manageable doses in the
same way that Mithridates could control his own intake of
poison but not that of his enemies. Just how art manages or
controls its potentially damaging content has been the subject of a great deal of modern psychoanalytic criticism, most
notably that of Holland. His view, as I have indicated, is that
the literary work, primarily through its aesthetic form but
also in its content, offers a massive set of defenses against the
anxiety which it arouses.[50]

In "Terence" there would appear to be a double set of
defenses at work, in the content and in the form. The intellectual content of the poem proposes a theory by which
poetry defends against the pain of life. The form of the poem
defends against the pain in other ways not suggested by the
content. More remarkably, it defends against the anxiety
aroused even by its own content. The lighthearted tone
serves to soften the impact of the pessimisitc view of life
contained in the poem's statement, to lessen the anxiety
generated by the philosophy that the world has "much less
good than ill" (l. 44), that "Luck's a chance, but trouble's
sure" (l. 46). The comic tone is in this manner a conscious

defense, a means of coping with painful experience (although it does not necessarily transpose the experience to one of pleasure). Ernst Kris has noted, in this regard, that "cheerful or comical effects can readily be put into the service of disguises of and defense against anxiety."[51] Such a view of humorous effects explains the discrepancy between theme and tone, but it also supports a further implication of "Terence," that the unique value of the mithridatic function of art is that it masters the painful nature of reality even as it reveals it. The poem's built-in defenses allow the reader to accept its painful conclusions without undue anxiety. This aspect of Housman's theory is not contained in the statement of the poem, but it is clearly suggested by the persona's attempt to defend against his harsh statement through humor. By this device human pain is transposed to a belly-ache, mortality to a dead cow, the foolish illusions of youth to an adolescent drinking bout. It is important to note that the humor neither denies the painful nature of life nor attempts to escape it, but it does help to render it acceptable. Lesser has made a similar point about comedy. He objects to "the common notion that what comedy supplies is escape, that it transposes us to a pleasurable artificial world which has no relevance for our everyday existence." He argues instead that we value comedy "because it supplies us with an attitude which is important, perhaps indispensable, for our survival in the world in which we live and err and suffer. . . . Without occasional recourse to that attitude, a creature like man, aspiring and god-like but also frail and fallible, might find it impossible to come to terms with himself."[52] It is possible, then, to see the comic mode of the poem not only as its primary strategy of defense but also as yet another means of returning the reader to reality by puncturing his illusions, reminding him of his human frailties.

Other defensive strategies of the kind identified by Holland are evident in "Terence,"[53] but at this point I am concerned with articulating Housman's theory rather than providing a reading of the poem. The theory itself seems to me of great consequence in reading all of Housman's poetry, as I will suggest in the chapter which follows. Furthermore, it casts new light on his description of the creation of his verse

in *The Name and Nature of Poetry*. The modern psychoanalytic theory which holds that literature serves as a
defense against pain or anxiety also holds that this defensive
aspect is essential to creativity, to the writer's commitment
to literature,[54] and Housman has provided an account of the
origin of his poetry which tallies almost perfectly with the
theory developed in "Terence."

In the Leslie Stephen Lecture, Housman describes the
composition of his poetry in terms that recall not only the
theme but also the imagery of the poem written more than
thirty-five years earlier. He likens his verse to "a morbid
secretion, like the pearl in the oyster," confides that "I have
seldom written poetry unless I was rather out of health," and
describes the experience, though pleasurable in part, as
"generally agitating and exhausting" (*SP*, p. 194). He adds
that if the poem "had to be taken in hand and completed by
the brain," it was "apt to be a matter of trouble and anxiety,
involving trial and disappointment" (*SP*, p. 195). As is the
case in "Terence," the lecture presents the creating of poetry
as a painful and anxious process associated with illness. It
also associates composition with oral imagery: the poems
were composed after "having drunk a pint of beer at luncheon," and the source of the poet's inspiration is identified
as "the pit of the stomach" (*SP*, p. 194). Since this activity
results in a "morbid secretion," we have, as Ernst Kris points
out, a description of the process of inspiration expressed in
oral, intestinal, and anal terms.[55] Kris, in fact, quotes approv-
ingly the whole of Housman's description of creation as a
classic statement of poetic inspiration given with "modera-
tion and prudence."[56] His careful analysis of the description
supports the view that Housman's account of the creation of
his own poetry is far from being the eccentric and thoughtless assertion of a classical scholar who strayed into the
foreign territory of literary criticism, the general attitude of
those who have responded to Housman's pronouncements
on the art of poetry. The parallel attitudes and images of
Housman's two accounts of his poetry, spaced over the
course of his career, lend additional evidence to the argument that the concepts of poetry in both "Terence" and *The
Name and Nature of Poetry* reflect the serious self-analysis

of a mind practiced in the reading and writing of poetry and candid in its response. And if Housman's self-analysis seems now to link him most closely with the psychoanalytic school, that should not be altogether surprising when we recall that the general theme of his public lecture is that poetry makes its appeal not to the intellect but "to something in man which is obscure and latent, something older than the present organization of his nature, like the patches of fen which still linger here and there in the drained lands of Cambridgeshire" (SP, p. 193).

## Notes

1. *The Letters of A. E. Housman*, p. 309.

2. In addition to *A. E. Housman: Selected Prose*, John Carter has edited *A. E. Housman: The Confines of Criticism* (Cambridge: University Press, 1969). The second volume is Housman's Cambridge Inaugural Address, delivered in 1911 and not published during his lifetime (because of his inability to verify a reference). The title was supplied by Carter.

3. Aristotle, *Poetics*, Chap. 4 in *Aristotle's Art of Poetry*, Ingram Bywater, trans., and W. Hamilton Fyfe, ed. (Oxford: Clarendon Press, 1940), p. 9.

4. Matthew Arnold, "Preface to *Poems* (1853)" in *The Portable Matthew Arnold*, ed. Lionel Trilling (New York: The Viking Press, 1949), p. 187.

5. *Poetics*, Chap. 4. p. 9.

6. Ibid., Chap. 4, p. 16.

7. "Preface to *Poems* (1853)," p. 186.

8. Ibid.

9. Ibid., p. 187.

10. One interpretation of the passage in Aristotle locates the carthartic effect within the structure of the work, not in the audience, though that is not the generally accepted view. For a survey of the various interpretations of the concept, see Gerald F. Else, *Aristotle's Poetics: The Argument* (Cambridge, Mass.: Harvard University Press, 1963), pp. 224–32.

11. I have argued at greater length for the idea that Terence clearly speaks for Housman, my assumption here, in *Housman's Land of Lost Content*, especially pp. 79–88.

12. It will be recalled that in *The Name and Nature of Poetry*

Housman located one of the seats of aesthetic sensation in the pit of the stomach (SP, p. 193).

13. Arnold's remarks were of course directed primarily to his own poem *Empedocles on Etna*, which he had omitted from the 1853 *Poems*.

14. Lionel Trilling, "Freud and Literature" in *The Liberal Imagination* (New York: The Viking Press, 1950), p. 56.

15. "Writers and Day-Dreaming" in *The Standard Edition of the Complete Psychological Works of Sigmund Freud*, ed. James Strachey (London: The Hogarth Press, 1959), 10:153. Hereafter cited as *Standard Edition*.

16. *Standard Edition*, 10:5.

17. Ibid., p. 23.

18. Ibid., p. 32.

19. Ibid., p. 35.

20. Freud's postulation of a death-wish as one consequence of the compulsion to repeat suggests a further parallel with the overall theme of Housman's poetry, but that is too large an issue to be dealt with here. A more detailed discussion of the death-wish in Freud and Housman follows in chapter 8.

21. "Freud and Literature," p. 56.

22. "The Dissection of the Psychical Personality," *Standard Edition*, 12:60. Neither could Housman escape what is universally known, and I am not arguing for the complete originality of his concept, although I have discovered no previous expression of it in the terms Housman employs. He may have been influenced by a passage in Book II of *Paradise Lost* in which the fallen angels steel themselves against their fate by composing painful songs of their present state and arguing the issues of fate, free will, and foreknowledge. Milton, however, makes clear that their attempts to defend against their condition are illusory:

> Vain wisdom all, and false philosophy!
> Yet with a pleasing sorcery could charm
> Pain for a while or anguish, and excite
> Fallacious hope, or arm the obdured breast
> With stubborn patience as with triple steel.
> [ll. 565–569]

Housman alludes to a passage immediately preceding this in the opening poem of *A Shropshire Lad*, and there are two other allusions to *Paradise Lost* in "Terence" (ll. 13 and 21–22). The poem may have also been influenced by Emerson's "Mithridates," two lines of which ("Give me agates for my meat; / Give me cantharids to eat") sound somewhat like ll. 69–70 of "Terence." Yet Emerson uses Mithridates for a role different from that assigned him by Housman; he is, for Emerson, the symbol of the man who finds virtue in all things. For an account of the post-Romantic tendency to deny pleasure as the essential element of literary response, see Lionel Trilling, "The Fate of Pleasure: Wordsworth to Dostoevsky" in *Romanticism Reconsidered,* ed. Northrop Frye (New York: Columbia University Press, 1963), pp. 73–106. Trilling emphasizes the importance of Dostoevsky and Freud in the modern repudiation of aesthetic pleasure. He does not mention Housman's concept, although it is a clearer instance of the tendency he is delineating than any he cites.

23. "Writers and Day-Dreaming," *Standard Edition,* 9:144.

24. "Psychopathic Characters on the Stage," trans. Henry Alden Bunker, *The Psychoanalytic Quarterly* 11 (1942): 459.

25. Ibid., pp. 459–60.

26. *Beyond the Pleasure Principle, Standard Edition,* 4:144.

27. Ibid.

28. "Psychopathic Characters on the Stage," p. 459.

29. "Writers and Day-Dreaming," *Standard Edition,* 9:159.

30. "Freud and Literature," p. 55.

31. Ibid., pp. 55–56.

32. *Psychoanalytic Explorations in Art* (New York: International Universities Press, 1952), pp. 210–11.

33. Ibid., p. 45.

34. *The Dynamics of Literary Response* (New York: Oxford University Press, 1968), p. 299. Holland defines a literary defense as "something that looks like such well-known [human] defenses as regression, isolation, reversal, and the like, although it is not an unconscious, automatic psychic mechanism like them but rather an explicit handling of an implicit fantasy." That is, a "defense mechanism" or "defensive mastery" in literature resembles particular unconscious defenses well known to psychoanalysts, but it occurs explicitly in the literary work as plot, character, or form (p. 106).

35. *Fiction and the Unconscious* (Boston: Beacon Press, 1957), pp. 130–131. Holland's statement is this: "Very loosely, then, we can say that form in a literary work corresponds to defense; content, to fantasy or impulse" (*The Dynamics of Literary Response,* p. 131).

36. *Fiction and the Unconscious,* p. 255.

37. Ibid., p. 259.

38. Ibid., pp. 258–59.

39. Ibid., p. 260. In *The Name and Nature of Poetry,* Housman does use the term *pleasure* in a general way both in relation to the reader's response and to the act of creation, but the term is qualified

both by the melancholy examples that Housman draws on for his "touchstones" and by the use of such other terms as *morbid, agitating, exhausting,* and *anxiety.* It is possible, perhaps, to argue that even anxiety and pain are ultimately pleasurable if they protect against greater pain, but that simply leads to a breakdown in our common use of these terms.

40. Holland's analysis of "Dover Beach" is found on pages 115–33 of *The Dynamics of Literary Response.* It has been reprinted in *Perspectives in Contemporary Criticism,* ed. Sheldon Norman Grebstein (New York: Harper and Row, 1968), pp. 248–67.

41. The term, as I have indicated above, was first used by Lionel Trilling in reference to Freud's ideas in *Beyond the Pleasure Principle.*

42. *The Dynamics of Literary Response,* p. 79. See Freud's "Writers and Day-Dreaming" (especially pp. 144, 153) for his own statement of this.

43. Holland, for example, points out a number of common associations between reading and eating, as when we call a man who "devours" books a "voracious" reader, or when Bacon tells us that "some books are to be tasted, others to be swallowed, and some few to be chewed and digested." We "hunger for knowledge" and "digest" the knowledge that we acquire (p. 75).

44. In an early draft of "Terence" Housman used the term *vaccination* in reference to his poetry. This may have led to the Mithridates allusion. Whatever the case, he canceled the line ("How well his vaccination took") and developed the Mithridates passage on the following page of the notebook. See Haber, *The Making of A Shropshire Lad,* pp. 314–15.

45. *Fiction and the Unconscious,* p. 260.

46. Ibid., p. 261.

47. See Sacvan Bercovitch, "Literature and the Repetition Compulsion," *College English* 29 (1968): 610. Bercovitch makes the same point in relation to Freud's theory in *Beyond the Pleasure Principle.*

48. *The Dynamics of Literary Response,* pp. 98–99.

49. Ibid., p. 99.

50. Almost the whole of *The Dynamics of Literary Response* is devoted to this theory, and any attempt to summarize it would lead to some oversimplification. However, a typical statement of Holland's view is this: "The unconscious fantasy at the core of a work will combine elements that could, if provided full expression, give us pleasure, but also create anxiety. It is the task of the literary 'work' to control the anxiety and permit at least partial gratification of the pleasurable possibilities in the fantasy. The literary work,

through what we have loosely termed 'form', acts out defensive maneuvers for us: splitting, isolating, undoing, displacing from, omitting (repressing or denying) elements of the fantasy" (p. 189). One basic difference between this concept and that articulated in "Terence," as I pointed out earlier, is Holland's insistence that the formal defenses transform the anxiety into pleasure; Housman implies that the aesthetic experience merely renders the anxiety bearable. This may be only a quibble with language, but it is an issue which must remain unresolved in the absence of more objective evidence. Holland acknowledges that "the question as to how a defense can reverse pain into pleasure reaches to the edge of psychoanalytic knowledge" (p. 299).

51. *Psychoanalytic Explorations in Art*, p. 146.

52. *Fiction and the Unconscious*, pp. 280–81.

53. Other common poetic defenses noted by Holland which may be located in the poem—rhythm, rhyme, sound, for example—are the common properties of all poetry. According to Holland, such elements "create an effect of logical inevitability, completeness, mastery, derived not from the sense of the words, but from their sound." They offer "a pseudo-solution at this surface level to the conflicts that adhere in the deeper content" (p. 146).

54. See, for example, *The Dynamics of Literary Response*, pp. 123–33.

55. *Psychoanalytic Explorations in Art*, p. 301.

56. Ibid., p. 295.

# 8
# CONCLUSION

OF THE PERSPECTIVES on his own art Housman has provided, none is more intriguing than Terence's psychologically oriented defense of his verse at the conclusion of *A Shropshire Lad*. Not only does it offer a justification for the despondent nature of the whole of Housman's poetry, but also it is now sanctioned by several decades of psychoanalytic theory and criticism, which it clearly anticipated. For once Housman cannot be accused of championing an old-fashioned conception of poetry; his defense is as novel as the latest study of Norman Holland. Yet significant questions remain unanswered. How seriously are we to regard a notion contained in one poem of *A Shropshire Lad*? That is, to what extent is the mithridatic principle consistent with what we already know of Housman's theory and practice of poetry?

In regard to this question, it may appear that in devoting a long chapter to the implications of one poem, however central, I have already been guilty of exaggerating the importance of what may have been no more than a moment's thought, and such might indeed be the case in a study of a poet like Yeats or Eliot who has provided ample evidence of his view of his own craft. But with a poet as reticent as Housman the commentator must take his evidence where he finds it, and any clue which may aid in reconstructing Housman's poetics deserves careful scrutiny. The final test of the importance of Housman's defense of his art lies, however, with the poetry itself. The crucial questions are these:

does the body of Housman's poetry support the theory contained in "Terence," and, even if it does, is the theory of any real value in establishing an approach to the poetry?

To answer these questions we may begin with a summary of the primary features of what I have been calling the mithridatic theory, as sketched by Housman in "Terence" and amplified by later psychoanalytic critics (following Freud, not Housman). The theory assumes first that the value of a despondent and pessimistic poetry such as that of Housman is to be found principally in its ability to immunize the reader against the certain and unalterable pain of life. By dealing imaginatively with experiences which are potentially painful, this sort of poetry strengthens our ability to cope with anxiety and pain. Its method of accomplishing this task is to be found both in its content, or discursive elements, and in its form, or nondiscursive elements. The content deals discursively with situations which arouse anxiety and thus allows us to confront and master these conflicts. The form serves in numerous ways to minimize the painfulness of the experience by providing defenses (analogous to the psychological defenses encountered in real life) which soften the mental anguish accompanying such confrontations. Whether the poem is actually able to transform anxiety or pain to pleasure is open to debate, although it may be only a semantic debate involving the term *pleasure*. At any rate, Housman's concept of the theory in "Terence" assumes that the poem does not attempt to eliminate the pain entirely; on the contrary, it requires that we experience a controlled amount of pain as defense against the much greater pain inherent in the nature of the world outside the poem.

Applying such a model to Housman's poems, we should expect to find a poetry whose subject matter is devoted primarily to the harshness of man's lot, the anxiety and pain that lie at the heart of life, and that is of course exactly what we encounter. So pervasively do the situations and conflicts which Housman chooses to dramatize involve the discovery of the hurtful nature of human existence that the theme has been the staple of Housman criticism since the publication of *A Shropshire Lad*. What is not so obvious is the manner in which Housman employs the nondiscursive elements of his poetry—form in the broadest sense of the term—to manage or control the potentially damaging content. It is here, I believe, in the analysis of aesthetic form, that the mithridatic principle proves most helpful in an approach to Housman, for it appears to offer a rationale for the characteristic features of his art. This argument may be demonstrated by looking at two of the best studies of Housman's style—those of Christopher Ricks and Randall Jarrell—in relation to the mithridatic theory.

Contemporary versions of the theory assume that artistic form works to defend against the anxiety aroused by the content, and that is the implication also of "Terence," although it is not stated directly. Norman Holland has provided the most detailed treatment of the manner in which form manages content, and he finds that the work's formal defenses, which soften the impact of the harsh content, may result in a discrepancy between a disturbing subject matter and a calming style.[1] That is, although we usually think of form as reinforcing content, in the case of a work of art devoted to a painful subject form may be used to mitigate, conceal, or deny the effect of the unpleasant theme. We have seen that in "Terence" such is the case, and it is not difficult to find the same discrepancy between subject matter and style repeated throughout the body of his poetry. Christopher Ricks has devoted an essay to this element of Housman's verse, and, as noted earlier, he argues that the most remarkable feature of the poems is the manner in which "rhythm and style temper or mitigate or criticise what in bald paraphrase the poem would be saying."[2] Although Ricks does not make a connection between the content-style discrepancy and Housman's defense in "Terence," his essay serves as the most cogent argument possible for a direct link between the mithridatic theory and the essential nature of Housman's poetry.

Rick's holds that although critics seem to take it for granted that Housman's poems endorse the pessimistic beliefs which they assert, such is often not the case, since the form of the poem is frequently at odds with what is being asserted. Rhythm and style never completely abolish the beliefs (they are not, in fact, abolishable), but they do temper them in that the movement of the poems tends to comment on, and alter, what they say. This effect, he finds, goes against a great deal of contemporary verse, where the form simply reinforces through its own medium what the diction is saying. By looking at examples from other poets quoted in *The Name and Nature of Poetry*, Ricks supports his contention that Housman was attracted to poetry which exhibited contrarieties and disparities of feeling, that is, an implied emotion running counter to that explicitly stated. He also gives a number of examples of this effect in Housman's own verse, one of which, Lyric VI of *More Poems*, I should like to discuss at greater length.

> I to my perils
> > Of cheat and charmer
> > Came clad in armour
> > > By stars benign.
> Hope lies to mortals
> > And most believe her,
> > But man's deceiver
> > > Was never mine.
>
> The thoughts of others
> > Were light and fleeting,
> > Of lovers' meeting
> > > Or luck or fame.
> Mine were of trouble,
> > And mine were steady,
> > So I was ready
> > > When trouble came.

This poem obviously serves well as an illustration of Ricks's notion of a disparity between what Housman's poetry says and how it says it. The poem, he finds, says a "dour glum cramping thing," but it says it with "gaiety and wit" that are "utterly inappropriate." In the midst of its pessimistic fortitude it has the effrontery to rhyme "charmer" and "armour"; its whole movement is that of the dance, "light and fleeting" rather than militant and grim, as its view of life would seem to require.[3] Most readers would agree, I think, that the charm of the poem derives from the fact that its form moves in a different direction from its paraphrasable statement and, further, that it is a more sophisticated and subtle poem because of this divergence. But what lies at the base of the cross-current of form and content? Ricks's only answer is that Housman was "fascinated" by such disparities and that he was drawn, perhaps unconsciously, to verse in which a submerged countercurrent of feeling vied with the more overt sentiment expressed. I should like to suggest that what we see here is the mithridatic principle at work, and a closer look at the poem should make that rather obvious.

The poem tells us that hope is a lier and a deceiver. Luck, fame, love are fleeting; only trouble is sure. This is certainly no comforting message, yet the effect of the poem is comforting, even cheery. Why? Because the form of the poem defends against its harsh content. Whatever anxiety we might otherwise feel in acknowledging the fate the poem predicts (a fate no intelligent person could deny) is tempered by the jauntiness of its movement, accented most perhaps by the short lines and feminine rhymes, as well as by the frequency of the rhymes. There is a sense in which the style of the poem is not appropriate, for it is almost as if the speaker were cheering himself up. Facing the worse that can happen to him, he has mastered it, and his mastery takes the form of gaiety. We may be reminded here of a better-known poem which suggests a variation of the mithridatic principle, Yeats's "Lapis Lazuli." Yeats reminds us, as does Housman, that art shows us the worst that life has to offer, "tragedy wrought to its uttermost," yet produces not hysteria but a kind of tragic joy:

> All perform their tragic play,
> There struts Hamlet, there is Lear,
> That's Ophelia, that Cordelia;
> Yet they, should the last scene be there,
> The great stage curtain about to drop,
> If worthy their prominent part in the play,
> Do not break up their lines to weep.
> They know that Hamlet and Lear are gay;
> Gaiety transfiguring all that dread.[4]

Yeats tells us of the gaiety that tragedy provides, yet the

movement of his poem is rather solemn, even bleak. Housman's language, on the other hand, offers us no relief from the steady march of "trouble," but his poem protects us against its perils in the same way the speaker is protecting himself. The speaker's defense is a simple one, comparable to the examples cited by Freud in *Beyond the Pleasure Principle* of children's games based on the child's worst fears, such as an absent father or a visit to the doctor. The motive for such play, as for Housman's poetic play, is to provide an opportunity for mastery of fear. In the poem, such mastery takes on the image of the speaker's being "clad in armour," and this is an apt image as well for the relationship of form and statement. The poem is also clad in armour, and its armour is its aesthetic form, which, however, shields us not only from what is outside but from what it covers, the poem's view of life. As a variation of the mithridatic theory of "Terence," the poem illustrates the manner in which art provides a defensive form for its potentially stressful content.

One might go further to suggest that the act of creating poetry was itself for Housman a means of mastery, a defense against anxiety. Such speculation is consistent with contemporary psychoanalytic literary theory as well as with the account in *The Name and Nature of Poetry* which characterizes the poetry as morbid and associates its creation with illness. However, that is a matter which is better left to the biographer and the Freudian critic. My concern is with Housman's theory and practice of poetry, and I am satisfied to argue here that whatever drive, conscious or unconscious, led Housman to poetry, the notion of poetry as defense which he articulates in "Terence" and illustrates masterfully in "I to my perils" is central to both his theory and practice and offers the best explanation for his attraction to a poetic style which appears at times to be at odds with his darkened view of life.

But what of that view of life itself? A second example may show how one further characteristic element of Housman's poetry—its preoccupation with death—is related to the mithridatic theory. R. P. Blackmur's statement that Housman wrote "almost entirely of death"[5] has been frequently echoed, usually as a part of a more general condemnation of his morbid subject matter. In what is perhaps the most highly regarded single essay on Housman,[6] Randall Jarrell reaches an interesting conclusion in regard to Housman's treatment of death in one typical poem, Lyric XVI of *A Shropshire Lad*. Here is the poem and a summary of Jarrell's argument.

> It nods and curtseys and recovers
>   When the wind blows above,
> The nettle on the graves of lovers
>   That hanged themselves for love.
>
> The nettle nods, the wind blows over,
>   The man, he does not move,
> The lover of the grave, the lover
>   That hanged himself for love.

Jarrell sees this as a quasi-philosophical poem meant to infect the reader with Housman's own belief. That belief involves a recognition of the painful and inescapable conditions of life, what Jarrell calls the "prosperous evil of the universe." By depicting a nettle as repeating over the grave, compelled by the wind of life, what the man in the grave did once when the gale of life blew through him, the poem implies that living is no more than a repetition of meaningless nodding actions, actions that haven't even the virtue of being our own (since the wind forces them out of us). But this general attitude toward life is complicated by the poem in a number of ways. There is irony in a nettle's dancing obliviously on the grave of a dead lover, for grass, as a symbol for transitoriness, here outlasts man. The fifth and sixth lines develop this paradox: a plant curtseys and nods, while the man, the most active of beings, cannot even move. This is the gloomy message of the poem, but there is also a sense of triumph, perhaps the ultimate triumph for man. He was once tossed about helplessly by the wind that blew through him; now the toughest of plants is more easily manipulated than he. To put it bluntly, death is better than life, and the recognition of this fact leads to the note of triumph in the poem.

Once we acknowledge this note of triumph, we may catch the ambiguity of the poem's conclusion; that is the possibility that it was the grave, not any living thing, for which the lover yearned and hanged himself. This is the logic which the poem requires, for hanging oneself for love of someone is absurd so far as furthering one's love, but if one is in love with death, suicide is the logical and obvious way to consummate that love. Of course the lover may have been deceived. He may have believed that he killed himself for love of someone, but the poem's implication is that the lover's one motive must have been the wish for death. Housman does not argue for the truth of that premise; he merely states it audaciously and innocently, as a fact as obvious as the other facts the poem presents about the wind, the nettle, and the grave.

It is a brilliant analysis, and having once seen the poem in this light I suspect no reader can ever read it in any other way. But I am primarily interested in following up some of the implications of Jarrell's reading in terms of the theory I have been pursuing. It is significant, first of all, that Jarrell speaks of the poem as designed to "infect" us with its belief. This term, which was apparently chosen innocently enough, takes us back to the immunization principle of "Terence"— the motive behind such a painful poem is the infection of the reader with a moderate case of the disease it protects him against. And what sort of protection does the poem offer? Jarrell correctly notes (while being apparently oblivious to the mithridatic theory) that the poem actually depicts a triumph, while it should, by all logic, depict only that which is most gloomy and mortifying to living creatures. Its ultimate triumph is to be found in the common wish for death.[7]

Here is another instance in which Housman gives us a full look at the worst, infects us with his own dark vision, yet manages to defend us against the anxiety of death and leaves us with a sense of victory. Jarrell sees all of this, yet because he is reading the poem in isolation and is apparently unwilling to credit Housman with any real knowledge of what he is up to, he reaches a rather odd conclusion in his final paragraph:

> Two of the generalizations carried over by this poem—that our actions are motivated by the wish for death, that our ostensible reasons for acts are merely rationalizations, veneers of apparent

motive overlying the real levels of motivation—are, in a less sweeping form, psychological or psychoanalytical commonplace today. But I am not going to hold up Housman's poem as a masterly anticipation of our own discoveries; so far as I can see, Housman was not only uninterested but incapable in such things, and pulled these truths out of his pie not because of wit, but because of the perverse and ingenious obstinacy that pulled just such gloomy judgments out of any pie at all. Here the shock and unlikeliness of what he said were what recommended it to him; and the discovery that these have been mitigated would merely have added to his gloom.[8]

Jarrell is rather too quick in dismissing Housman from his own poem. In the manner of the New Critics, he tends to appropriate the poem to himself, taking credit for its more interesting discoveries. Yet we have already seen that Housman was certainly not uninterested in such things, and the poem itself is ample proof that he was not incapable. It is rather ironic that Jarrell should have demonstrated the brilliance of the poem's insights into human motivation only to dismiss the poet as a victim of perversity and obstinacy. And his final assertion that Housman would have been vexed to discover that the gloomy judgments of the poem had been mitigated by its subtle and ambiguous implications is certainly wrong. It should be clear by this point that one common pattern of Housman's poetry is the tendency of one element of the poem to mitigate or deny what another asserts.

Perhaps the most interesting implication of Jarrell's analysis is his treatment of the death-wish contained in the poem, especially since the wish for death is such a pervasive property of Housman's verse. Jarrell recognizes that Housman anticipated Freud in this discovery, but he obviously regards it as an accident, something pulled out of a pie. The truth is that the wish for death, as a defense, is a logical extension of the mithridatic theory. It may be remembered that it was in Freud's own version of this theory in *Beyond the Pleasure Principle* that the death-wish made its first appearance in his metapsychological writings.

It would at first seem inconsistent that a mental process which seeks to protect the mind from anxiety and pain should culminate in a wish for death, itself a source of great anxiety. Yet in *Beyond the Pleasure Principle* Freud pursues a line of speculation which leads directly to this conclusion. After postulating that there exists in the mind a compulsion to repeat unpleasant experiences for the purpose of mastery, Freud argues that this compulsion is something derived from the most intimate nature of the instincts:

> But how is the predicate of being "instinctual" related to the compulsion to repeat? At this point we cannot escape a suspicion that we have come upon the track of a universal attribute of instincts and perhaps of organic life in general which has not hitherto been clearly recognized or at least not explicitly stressed. *It seems, then, that an instinct is an urge inherent in organic life to restore an earlier state of things* which the living entity has been obliged to abandon under the pressure of external disturbing forces; that is, it is a kind of organic elasticity, or, to put it another way, the expression of the inertia inherent in organic life.[9]

By postulating that instincts are an expression of the conservative nature of living substance and tend toward a restoration of an earlier state of things and, further, that the phenomena of organic development must be attributed to external disturbing and diverting influences, Freud is able to specify the final goal of all organic striving:

> It would be in contradiction to the conservative nature of the instincts if the goal of life were a state of things which had never yet been attained. On the contrary, it must be an *old* state of things, an initial state from which the living entity has at one time or other departed and to which it is striving to return by the circuitous paths along which its development leads. If we are to take it as a truth that knows no exception that everything living dies for *internal* reasons—becomes inorganic once again—then we shall be compelled to say that 'the aim of life is death' and, looking backwards, that '*inanimate things existed before living ones*'.[10]

Freud is aware that this assumption of an instinctive death-wish must appear bewildering to the reader who is accustomed to thinking of instincts as self-preservative. He theorizes, however, that the instincts of self-preservation are "component instincts whose function it is to assure that the organism shall follow its own path to death, and to ward off any possible ways of returning to inorganic existence other than those which are immanent in the organism itself. . . .

What we are left with is the fact that the organism wishes to die only in its own fashion."[11]

Lionel Trilling argues that, in terms of Freud's contribution to literature, the idea of the death instinct, along with the concurrent notion of the "reality" or mithridatic principle, forms the "crown of Freud's broader speculation on the life of man." These theories, he believes, hold great promise for the artist because "the Freudian man is . . . a creature of far more dignity and far more interest than the man which any other modern system has been able to conceive."[12] No one is apt to make the same claim for Housman's conception of man. We have already seen that Jarrell is not quite willing to believe that Housman understood fully the presence of the Freudian death-wish in his poetry. Yet it is surely no accident that the two lines of speculation pursued by Freud and Housman led them to the same conclusion. Freud's assumption of a repetition-compulsion which creates apprehension for defensive purposes led him to the notion of an instinctive desire to return to an inorganic state. Pursuing the same defensive strategy two decades earlier, Housman was similarly confronted with the notion of a desire for death as an emblem of man's triumph over the pain of living, a triumph which, Jarrell reminds us, is "the most absolute that man can know." In terms of the mithridatic theory in Housman's poetry, then, the death-wish is the ultimate defense, the mental conception which is most successful in hardening us against anxiety and pain and which is apt to be employed when anxiety and pain are most intense.

There is one obvious difference between Freud's conception of the death-wish as a part of the mithridatic principle and that of Housman. Freud, of course, is investigating these phenomena on an instinctive, unconscious level; Housman's pre-Freudian poetry advances them to the level of the conscious mind. Yet since defense against pain and the wish for death are themselves frequently the subjects of the poems, it could hardly be any other way. A Freudian critic could doubtless ferret out further unconscious death wishes in Housman's poetry, but that would say no more about his understanding of the idea than could be said about any other poet. It is the fact that Housman consciously employs the death-wish as a part of the broader defensive strategy of his poetry which strengthens my belief that his conception of the therapeutic value of painful poetry embodies essentially the theory advanced by Freud twenty years later, which Trilling sees as crowning his speculations on the life of man.

The discussions of Ricks and Jarrell demonstrate how pervasively Housman's conception of poetry as defense affected his verse, and the examples are the more persuasive because neither critic pursued his analysis with my ulterior motive. Neither, that is, recognized a connection between the elements of Housman's poetry he was attempting to isolate and an artful and conscious strategy on Housman's part. Once we recognize the possibility of such a strategy, we may begin to see other characteristics of the poetry in terms of the defensive theory. Housman's choice of the naive persona, for example, seems to be a part of his more general tendency to counter the reader's innocence and thus inure him to a painful reality. From this point of view, the first half of *A Shropshire Lad* shows us the awakening of the innocent to the burden of being human; the second half (and most of the remainder of the poetry) presents innumerable means of coping with this burden. *A Shropshire Lad* culminates in the explanation for the whole poetic process, stated in its final two poems.[13] The structural patterns of the poems also devise ways of revealing to the innocent persona moments of painful insight or, conversely, steeling him against these perceptions. The rhythms of the verse, moreover, may be seen not only as controlling the voice of the naive persona but also as defending against the anxiety-producing content by introducing a music which runs counter to the poems' explicit statements. Other possibilities present themselves, and it would seem fundamental that any study of Housman's poetic technique take into account the mithridatic principle which he announced as the basis for his poetry.

Such observations regarding style and technique are perhaps obvious, and they are offered here not so much as new insights into Housman's poetry as confirmations of the efficacy of the conception of poetry which he appears to have held at the time when the most of his verse was written. Neither am I suggesting that we are obliged to read Housman's verse in the same light in which he apparently regarded it. Housman reminds us in *The Name and Nature of Poetry* of the limitations of criticism and of the dangers of confusing personal opinions and objective truth. Throughout this study my aim has been to open up new possibilities in reading Housman rather than to argue one approach to his poetry, and my principal aim has been the revaluation of Housman as an artist. I believe that the views expressed at the beginning of his poetic career in his own verse and at the end of his career in *The Name and Nature of Poetry* give evidence of a thoughtful and provocative theory of poetry which furnished the basis for his own poetic practice. His conception of poetry is not inconsistent with his own verse, as we have been led to believe, and is no more old-fashioned than that of Eliot. He anticipated a great deal of what we now regard as fresh and innovative, and I suspect that even the severe limitations which he placed on the critic's function will come to be seen more and more as central to our view of the work of criticism.

## Notes

1. Holland makes this point most forcefully in his lengthy analysis of "Dover Beach" (*The Dynamics of Literary Response,* pp. 115–33). He argues that the form of the poem serves as a denial of its anxiety-arousing content. The resulting effect he labels "reassurance-through-disillusion" (p. 291). The entire discussion of "Dover Beach" should be of interest to the reader who wishes to pursue the methodology involved in the analysis of the defensive strategies offered by aesthetic form. My concern here is with the general implications of the theory and not with the specific methods of this type of psychoanalytic criticism.

2. "The Nature of Housman's Poetry," p. 106.

3. Ibid., p. 108.

4. *The Collected Poems of W. B. Yeats* (New York: Macmillan, 1956), p. 292, ll. 9–17.

5. *The Expense of Greatness* (Gloucester, Mass.: Peter Smith, 1958), p. 202.

6. "Texts from Housman," *Kenyon Review* 1 (1939): 260–71. Ricks says that this is "still easily the best discussion of Housman"

(p. 119). The essay deals with two poems, *More Poems* XXIII and *A Shropshire Lad* XVI. I am concerned here only with the second, but its conclusion is echoed by the first, as Jarrell points out.

7. Jarrell also finds the death-wish in a more sublimated form in the other poem he discusses, "Crossing alone the nighted ferry."

8. "Texts from Housman," p. 271.

9. *Standard Edition*, 18:36; Freud's italics. My brief summary does not do justice to the subtlety of Freud's argument.

10. Ibid., p. 38; Freud's italics.

11. Ibid., p. 39.

12. "Freud and Literature," pp. 56–57.

13. See *Housman's Land of Lost Content*, pp. 88–90 for a discussion of the view of his poetry Housman presented in the final lyric of *A Shropshire Lad*. Essentially, Housman's argument is that the value of his verse lies in its ability to transcend his own mutable state and so to strengthen future generations of readers "When I am dead and gone."

# Index

157